AYR remembered

Denholm Reid & Ken Andrew

FURTHER READING

The books listed below were used by the authors during their research. None of them are available from Stenlake Publishing. Those interested in finding out more are advised to contact their local bookshop or reference library.

Ken Andrew, *Guide to Kyle & Carrick District*, 1981.
Rob Close, *Ayrshire & Arran – An Illustrated Architectural Guide*, 1992.
John Strawhorn, *The History of Ayr*, 1989.

ACKNOWLEDGEMENTS

The authors wish to thank Bob Blane, Georgie and Peter Blane, William Bennet, Ronnie Brash and the staff of Ayr Carnegie Library for the information they provided, and their wives, Deirdre Reid and Sheena Andrew, for their unstinting support.

Original photographs by Ken Andrew appear on the front/back cover and pages 1, 8 (lower), 12, 14 (both), 15 (upper), 16 (lower), 18 (upper), 19 (centre), 21 (lower), 22 (both), 23 (lower), 25 (lower), 26 (lower right), 27 (lower left), 28/29 (all), 30 (lower), 32/33 (lower), 34/35, 38 (lower), 39 (both), 40 (upper), 50 (upper), 52 (lower), 53 (both), 54/55, 56 (upper), 57 (both), 58 (inset), 60/61 (lower), 62/63 (all), 65 (lower), 69, 74 (both), 76 (both), 78 (lower), 79 (upper and lower left), 80 (both), 81 (both), 83 (lower), 84/85, 86/87 (all), 88 (centre and lower), 91 (lower), 92/93 (both) and 94/95 (both). The remaining illustrations are from the collection of Denholm Reid, with the exception of the adverts on pages 5, 11 and 15 which appear courtesy of Donald McIver, and the photograph on page 50 (lower) which appears courtesy of W.A.C. Smith.

The background of this view from 1937 is dominated on the right by the gasometer and associated buildings of the gasworks, to the left of which are the Barracks (in the middle) and the shipyard. Overlooking the putting green is the back of the houses on Queen's Terrace. The entire background has altered drastically today with blocks of flats and the Citadel Leisure Centre dominating the scene.

Previous page: The impressive entry to Ayr town centre from the north across the New Bridge. The character of the scene is greatly enhanced by the double bow-fronted building to the left and the bowed building on the right. Incredibly, the town came near to demolishing this entry in the 1960s for less imaginative developments similar to the plain Woolworth's building on the left. Conservationists forced a rethink. This view from the roof of the Carnegie Library looks down on a four-way junction which often required the control of a policeman. River Street has now been closed off where the Kilmarnock Equitable Co-operative Society van is emerging, and other restrictions have been imposed on traffic. When this photograph was taken in the 1970s, the Co-operative Permanent Building Society still occupied the bowed building.

FOREWORD

This book takes the form of several tours in and around the Auld Toon, stopping off with the help of contemporary pictures to look at various aspects of Ayr life in the twentieth century. Included are scenes around the town which Ken Andrew recorded with his camera from the 1950s to the 1990s, while I have amassed a large collection of postcards and printed material covering the earlier part of the century. Sadly, during the writing of this book, Ken passed away. My thanks are due to his wife Sheena for her continued support and encouragement with this project.

Denholm Reid,
November 2001.

Miss Bessie Greenhill's Orchestra, here pictured in their broderie anglaise outfits, was one of the string groups that were once popular at the Banks o' Doon Tea Gardens.

The first sight which greets
visitors arriving by train at
Ayr Station is Burns Statue
Square. Were they to climb on
to the roof of the Station Hotel
the view would not be too
dissimilar to this early 1940s
view. While the traffic layout
has changed considerably,
most of the buildings are
recognisable, although with
changed identities.
Immediately it is obvious that
the 'square' is more of a right-
angled triangle, with the
Odeon cinema on the shortest
side, shops on the longest side,
and on the third, Killoch Place,
Miller Road leads off, with the
British Linen Bank, Britannic
Assurance Co. and Beresford
Temperance Hotel (at one time

there were seven temperance hotels in Ayr, all situated close to the station and harbour). This area had been known as the
Townhead and was the site of the town's cattle and horse markets. The opening of Ayr Townhead railway station in 1857
(which stood a few yards from the position of the current Ayr Station) led to the creation of Miller Road, Beresford Terrace
and other residential streets. The cattle market moved to a site beyond the railway and in 1892 the Burns statue was
unveiled. The triangular space then took on a new life as Burns Statue Square.

The bronze statue of Robert Burns was presented to the town by Ayr Burns Club in front of a vast crowd. It is mounted on
a granite pedestal on which are bronze plaques depicting scenes from his life and poems. The impressive ironwork
railings were regrettably removed during the 1940s, supposedly to help the war effort, and were never replaced.

The buildings on the left of the Square have not altered much in profile, although few contain the same businesses today. In the background, to the right of the Burns statue, can be seen the entrance to the Union Arcade, a lane which runs from the Square to Smith Street. Union Buildings, built *c*.1890, was the name given to the properties on the Square and Smith Street which backed on to the lane.

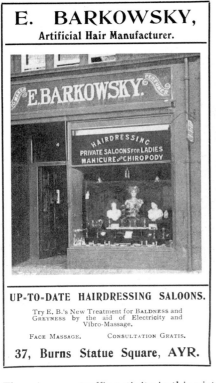

There is more traffic activity in this picture from the 1920s. The Odeon cinema and surrounding garages had not yet been built to the south of the Square. The skyline is dominated by the French Renaissance-style Station Hotel which opened in June 1886, having taken three years to build. The architect was Andrew Galloway, Chief Engineer of the Glasgow & South Western Railway Company; interestingly, this is the only building he is known to have designed. In front of the hotel is the South African War Memorial which was erected in tribute to Royal Scots Fusiliers who lost their lives in various South African conflicts between 1879 and 1902. *Left:* An advert for one of the businesses of Burns Statue Square which appeared in an 'Official Guide' to the town from 1910.

5

By 1952, when this photograph was taken, some major changes had taken place in the Square, notably in the 'island' where the South African War Memorial was incorporated in an elongated section east of the main Burns statue area. The new layout, which opened the year before, was described in a local newspaper as 'an eyesore'. To the right of the Station Hotel, just visible beyond the railway bridge is the Market Inn which was built in 1910. Particularly conspicuous are the Western S.M.T. buses which provided local and out-of-town services.

Souvenir
of the *Opening*

ODEON
THEATRE Regd

AYR   JULY 30TH. 1938

Dominating the south side of the Square is the Odeon cinema which was opened in July 1938 by the local MP, Sir Thomas Moore. The programme on the opening evening included a musical interlude with band and pipers, British news, Walt Disney's latest cartoon *Donald's Better Self*, and the film *The Prisoner of Zenda*, starring Ronald Colman and Madeleine Carroll.

6

Burns Statue Square, looking from the top of Dalblair Road in 1952. Dominating the background behind the Odeon cinema is the massive ice rink fronting on to Beresford Terrace. The stylish building incorporating the Athole Arms Bar in the left foreground was designed by William Cowie and built in 1900. The scene is quite different today. Vehicles approaching from the south and west now sweep clockwise around the square and behind the Odeon down Parkhouse Street, in effect forming a giant roundabout, while the road in front of the Odeon and Burns Statue has become a cul-de-sac with parking. The garages flanking the Odeon are gone and Burns House, a tall ungainly office block now owned by the local council, occupies ground to the left of the cinema. The ice rink has also gone, having been replaced by a Safeway store which later moved to the other side of the railway.

Looking along Killoch Place, on the west side of Burns Statue Square, towards Alloway Place sometime either in late 1924 or early the following year. The picture can be dated with some certainty as the tram poles which stood in the centre of the road have been removed and car no. 20 is still open-topped (it was later given a roof). Prominent on the top of the Union House building is a sign for Morgenthaler, hairdresser.

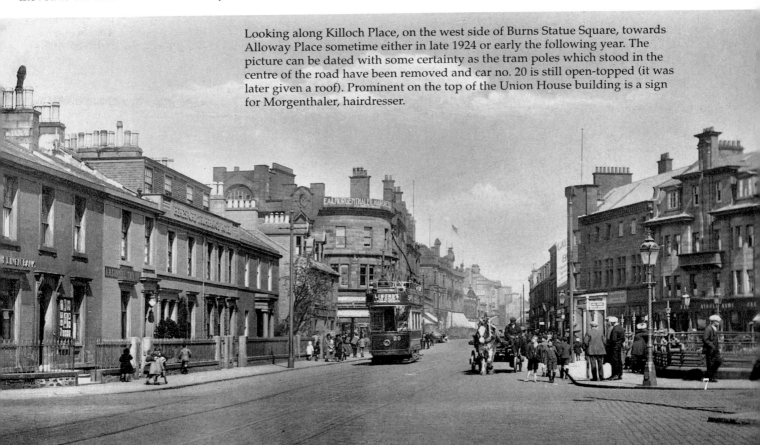

This postcard, sent in 1916, looks down Alloway Street from Burns Statue Square. At the corner with Dalblair Road on the left is Anderson Brothers of Union House, drapers and milliners. The prominent red sandstone building on the right was initially used as a drill hall by the Royal Scots Fusiliers and in 1909 became Ayr's first cinema, the Palace. In the left background is the recently built Hourston's store. This area is recognisable today although with many changed names and considerable alterations in the road layout.

In 1925 Ben Popplewell & Co. bought the Gaiety Theatre and the Palace cinema and let out the latter as a ballroom. Bobby Jones took over the ballroom in 1935 and remained proprietor until April 1965 when he retired. A native of Glasgow, Jones already owned a ballroom in the city before he bought the Ayr premises. He later became an Ayr town councillor. The ballroom was very popular during the Second World War and was known to get a bit too lively at times when young men on leave from the army, navy and air force competed with GIs from the USAF base at Prestwick for the attention of the local girls. Later, the premises became a bingo hall, then an amusement arcade, and is now a night club. The towered block was built in red sandstone in 1901 and designed by the talented local architect, James A. Morris. This picture dates from 1980.

Dalblair House was built in 1795 for James Gibb, a local industrialist. One hundred years later the mansion house was converted into a hotel. On its opening a local paper waxed lyrically on its features – 'The front entrance from Alloway Street is very elegant, two pillars of grey granite being exceedingly striking', while its hall was 'far and away the best in town'. Over the years the Hotel Dalblair, as it was known, underwent a number of alterations and extensions (this view from early last century is before one such extension), and achieved four-star status. Many famous names stayed at the Dalblair when appearing locally, including Harry Lauder, Will Fyffe and Renee Houston. With the changing demands of visitors and limitations for further improvement, its doors closed for the last time in November 1961. Plans were announced to demolish the hotel and replace it with a new six-storey one, a precinct of thirty shops, a supermarket and offices. The hotel was duly demolished and made way for the shopping development of Dalblair Arcade, now known as the Arran Mall, and an extension to Hourston's department store. A section of balustrade, which came from the New Bridge and which was incorporated into the building of the hotel, is now all that remains of it and can be seen above Logan the Jeweller and adjacent shops.

For over a hundred years the name of Hourston's has been known to Ayr townspeople as the department store at the 'top of the town', where they could buy everything from clothes to china, haberdashery to pots and pans, and have lunch or afternoon tea, view mannequin parades, have their hair styled, or, at the appropriate time of the year, visit Santa in his 'grotto'. In the late 1880s David Hourston, who had arrived from Orkney, opened a shop in Kyle Street. Such was his success that he built and established a new shop in Alloway Street in 1896 and took in his two sons as partners. Thus began the firm of D. Hourston & Sons. On David's death in 1917 the sons took over the business, which had become one of the largest retail drapery establishments in Scotland. Its tearooms, smoking rooms and roof gardens became famed across the country. In April 1949 the business was acquired by the House of Fraser group and in the years following this various changes took place, both in name (it became 'Arnott's' for a time) and again in ownership. Happily, the original name is now restored and Hourston's remains one of the busiest stores in Ayr.

Taken in the early years of the last century this view of the High Street is from the foot of Kyle Street close to the junction with Alloway Street. The railings of the subterranean gentlemen's public convenience are on the extreme left. Also on the left is the Plough Inn. The Windsor Restaurant on the right was run by P. Andreoli, 'formerly at the Station Hotel Ayr, and the Grand Comedy Restaurant, London'. A speciality was tripe soup and dressed tripe, and as well as providing breakfasts, luncheons, teas, dinners and suppers, 'picnics, soirees, dinner parties, etc. [were] purveyed for at strictly moderate charges'. Next door up the street was Wm. McCance, newsagent, while down the street were the draper's premises of Hyslop, Wallace & Co.

To Burnsians the world over the Tam o' Shanter Inn and the Auld Brig are second only in importance to Burns Cottage itself. There was a public house on this site in the High Street in the mid-eighteenth century and it was rebuilt some fifty years later; a landlord later saw the benefits of claiming its association with Burns's epic poem. The property changed hands a number of times before the town council purchased it in the 1930s. They leased it as a public house until the mid-fifties when it was converted into a museum, although it reverted to its former use in 1994.

An advert for Howat's ironmongers from the 1910 'Official Guide', along with a bill from the shop.

The Wallace Tower was designed by Thomas Hamilton, the architect of the Town Buildings. Built in 1834, to replace an earlier tower on the same site, it stands 115 feet high and has a hall suite behind, added in the 1880s. Its name may be connected to the Wallaces of Craigie, but it has become more associated with William Wallace whose statue fills a space in the front, this being best seen from across the street. The presence of tramcar no. 21 in this High Street shot of 1924 suggests that it was a race day, possibly the September Gold Cup day. The double deck car seated twenty-three on the lower deck and thirty-nine on the top and was bought specifically for use on the Hawkhill section (Racecourse route) of the tramways.

Taken from the top of the Wallace Tower, this photograph from 1967 looks north down the High Street to the Winton Buildings where the street narrows. The Gaumont, one of six cinemas in Ayr at the time, is prominent in the foreground. Western S.M.T. buses are conspicuous and car traffic light. Increasing congestion later brought about a ban on cars and a partially pedestrianised scheme. The town steeple dominates the scene.

This view west from the Wallace Tower dates from the early 1920s. Travelling south-west along Carrick Street (just right of centre bottom) the Gaiety Theatre can be seen on the right hand side at the junction with Boswell Park. Along a bit, running diagonally to the right, is Barns Street leading down to Wellington Square, and just discernible beyond is the dome of the County Buildings. The foreground left area comprising the back of High Street, Carrick Street and Dalblair Road, has changed considerably. Gone is the sprawl of factories which have been replaced by the Kyle Centre, a multi-storey car park, office buildings and the Jarvis International Hotel (previously called the Caledonian Hotel).

Looking up the High Street, and again the Wallace Tower dominates the scene. The prominent Grecian-styled building on the left was built in 1856 and housed the Union Bank. Today it houses the Halifax. A little further up on the same side is Hepworth the tailors and Boots the chemist, which is still there. Across the road, on the right hand side, is the Picture House (later the Gaumont) which opened in 1921. It has since been replaced by Littlewoods' store. The architecture on this side contrasts disappointingly with that of the other side which still has some fine features above street level.

13

The Butter Market Hall Close on the High Street, pictured in 1975. This gave access to the public toilets and the billiard saloon beyond. In the past various locations were set aside for particular markets. A butter market was established in Newmarket Street in 1814, but was moved to this site in 1869. British Home Stores has since redeveloped the site, retaining the upper three storeys of the sandstone facade.

The *Ayr Advertiser* was founded in 1803 and is Ayrshire's oldest newspaper. Its offices are now in Fort Street, but pictured here, before the move, is the Reporters' Room at 100 High Street. The paper was printed in the building behind the Reporters' Room until the owners sold out to the Guthrie Group who began printing it in Ardrossan. The stone above the doorway is one of four from the original New Bridge over the River Ayr and depicts the burgh seal. The high building on the right was used latterly by Callan's auctioneers, but the whole site has now been redeveloped as shops.

A lengthy queue stretches from McCall the baker's past the Auld Hoose and up Hope Street behind the Clydesdale Bank in the High Street. The cause of the queuing was a strike by local van drivers in 1970 which led to a shortage of bread.

Hope Street runs down from the High Street behind the Winton Buildings (now the premises of the Clydesdale Bank) and the site of the medieval tolbooth (now shops), rejoining the High Street at the Fish Cross. Since it makes these buildings resemble an island in the High Street it was once known as Isle Lane and is still known popularly as the 'Back o' the Isle'. This view from around 1875 looks down towards the Fish Cross from Newmarket Street. On the right is the Wallace Tavern (not named after the patriot, but instead the proprietor Joseph Wallace), which shortly afterwards became the premises of Wallace Allan, watchmaker and jeweller, previously based at 91 High Street, and still in business today.

An open-top tram trundles up the High Street towards the Kirkport. On the left are the prominent Winton Buildings which were built in 1844 on the site of the old meal market. They were named in honour of the Earl of Eglinton and Winton, who was Lord Lieutenant of the county at the time. Jutting out further down at the corner of Newmarket Street and High Street is a baronial-style building erected in 1886. On the front of it a statue of William Wallace occupies a niche at the first floor level, although it had to have its legs shortened to fit.

Shining Belisha beacons add to the reflections in the wet High Street in this 1950s view from Old Bridge Street. The plaque above the doorway on the right identifies this space as the site of the Fish Cross where the fish market was once held. A sculpture of a fisherman holding 'the last fish' has since also been installed to mark the historic site. The hinged circular 'no waiting this side today' sign on the lamp-post on the right – which was obviously being ignored – was an early attempt to control parking.

High Street, looking towards the Sandgate from where it curves close to the Fish Cross, 1903. Prominent in the foreground is the grocer and wine merchant Robert Forrest & Co. who was established in 1828. Around 1910 he advertised his own product 'The Forrest, an original blend of some of the best Scottish whiskies, 7 years old speciality recommended, price 18/6d. per gallon'. At the corner with Old Bridge Street is James Smith & Son ('cash drapery warehouse, costume, dress and mantle-making, blouses and boleros'). Above the shopfront is a bracket which held wires for the tramway cables. These brackets can still be seen on some buildings in the High Street. A sign on the lamp standard points to the Ayr Coffee House, while a tram makes its way up the street, the tramway having been opened just two years previously.

Looking up the High Street from the Malt Cross on a busy Saturday in 1939, there is no shortage of buses coming down. The bus stop today is in much the same position as then. The gap site on the left had only just appeared with the demolition of the building there, which contained empty shops, the previous year. On the left hand side of the street a van belonging to the Gilchrist Land o' Burns Bakery is parked outside Robert Sharp & Co., drapers, which was next door to F. W. Woolworth & Co., whose premises occupied the site of the Kings Arms Hotel when it was demolished some fourteen years previously. Beyond this are a printers and stationers, and a music-sellers, and then the premises of Montague Burton Ltd, tailors, followed by Marks & Spencer with its clock prominently displayed. Further on there's Lipton's, provision merchants, and disappearing towards the bend, Logan the jeweller and the Dorris Tearooms. On the other side of the street, heading back down, is Brown Bros., fishmongers, Afflecks, house furnishers, John P. Williamson, butchers, and a little further on, past a tobacconist and chemist, there is the Registrar's Office, council offices, and Robert Wallace the grocer and wine merchant. Of all the businesses in this scene, few remain today, notably Woolworth's, while Marks & Spencer have moved further up the street

17

Opposite:

Upper: By 1969 modern projecting signs were altering the facades of the High Street shops. Marks & Spencer were still occupying their old store behind the clock, but later moved on to a vast new building to the right beyond the gap of Old Bridge Street. An indoor market called the Forum now occupies the old site. Woolworth's stands on the site of the King's Arms Hotel, which closed in 1924, with Alexander Fergusson's printing office, now closed, to the right. Marks & Spencer's store was opened in May 1935 and had some twenty departments selling a wide variety of goods among which no single item cost more than five shillings! Staff welfare was considered an integral part of the company's policy; an article in the *Ayrshire Post* about the opening of the store reported that employees, who worked a forty-eight hour week with a morning off each month, had their own restaurant which offered two-course lunches costing 6*d.* and a rest room in which they could 'spend the leisure time that remains between the finish of their meals and the recommencement of duties'.

Lower: A single deck A.A. bus picks up passengers in the Sandgate at the stop opposite the fire station. Just out of view in the foreground, stones are set in the roadway marking the position of the Malt Cross which stood there from the time of Charles II until 1778 when it was removed on the building of the first New Bridge. This was a replica of the Market Cross of Edinburgh and was ostensibly the buying and selling point for malt, although this occurred in other parts of the town as well. Safety rails had not yet been erected at the crossings at the junction. Who, especially cyclists, can forget the cobbles up the Sandgate? The main entrance to the town buildings is on the left (with a lamp outside it). These were built around 1830 in the classical style popular at the time. The buildings' slim tapering steeple rises to a height of 225 feet, making it visible from miles around. A hall was added along the High Street around 1880, and following a fire in 1897 the interior of the building was reconstructed. The town hall has been used for many events over the years including concerts, conferences and exhibitions.

The Scots-born tenor Kenneth McKellar acknowledges the applause after performing a selection of Scots songs with the Scottish National Orchestra in Ayr Town Hall in 1957. Over the years concerts have been held in the town hall by local organisations such as the Ayr Amateur Orchestra (now Ayrshire Symphony Orchestra), the Ayr Choral Union and Ayr Burgh Choir, while national orchestras that have played there have included the Scottish National (formerly known as the Scottish Orchestra and now called the Royal Scottish National Orchestra) and the BBC Scottish. It is also a venue for many of the events of the annual Ayrshire Music Festival.

THE SANDGATE & TOWN STEEPLE, AYR.

From earliest times the Sandgate has been one of Ayr's main thoroughfares. Its buildings date from the fifteenth century Lady Cathcart's House at the junction with Cathcart Street, to the twentieth century post office at the Boswell Park corner, but the rest are predominantly Georgian and Victorian. Many of the shops in this mid-1930s picture had been there from the early years of the century and were to remain until the 1950s and '60s. On the east side of the street there was Stephen & Pollock, booksellers and stationers, Grant & Watson, outfitters, Laurie & Smith, drapers and dressmakers, and further along, Afflecks, house furnishers, Wm. Auld, china merchants, and Littlejohn Brothers, wine merchants, whose wine cellars were reputed to have once been the dungeons of the Old Tolbooth. In the midst of this stretch was the Fire Station which was based there from 1930 until the new fire station opened on the site of the former Content House in 1963. On the opposite side of the road, going down towards New Bridge Street, there was Thomas Samson, grocer, and the Bank of Scotland. At the corner of Cathcart Street where the Sandgate narrows was G. & T. Girdwood, bakers, which adjoined the premises of the 'Pru' (Prudential), and further down is 'Billy' Bridges Bar.

Opposite: The Western S.M.T. bus station at the top of the Sandgate, with the former Green's Playhouse Cinema behind. Stagecoach later took over the station and made considerable alterations to ease congestion. The entrance from Boswell Park (top left) was closed off and all buses now enter from Douglas Street (top right) with more space created by the removal of the narrow shelters. This 1972 photograph was taken from the roof of Wellington Chambers at the corner of Fullarton Street and the Sandgate. In the early 1920s several firms operated charabancs in and around Ayr mostly for private hire, for excursions, or from the villages around Ayr on Saturdays and market days. From 1923 Ayr & District Motor Services and the Scottish Transport Co. ran regular services to Ayr from outlying towns, and in 1924 a depot was opened in the Sandgate. Operating between Ayr and Glasgow in the 1920s and 1930s were John C. Sword's Midland buses and O'Hara's Southern buses. In the late 1920s several local bus companies started up and even the owner of the Glen Tearooms in Longhill Avenue ran a service named 'The Land o' Burns'. In 1930 some smaller operators formed A.A. Motor Services Ltd with a depot in Boswell Park and the following year the Scottish Motor Traction Co., who provided tramway replacement services after the tramway closed, bought out the remaining competitors. In 1932 Western S.M.T. was formed as the south-west subsidiary of the S.M.T.

Ayr Skating Rink, where locals came not to enjoy ice-skating, but roller skating which was once a popular recreation. This building, with its highly ornate front, stood in what later became Boswell Park. Its popularity waned with the arrival of the movies and it shut in 1910, although it soon reopened as a picture house. After the First World War it became Green's Playhouse, showing silent films accompanied by a cinema orchestra. In September 1929, shortly after the introduction of the 'talkies', it burned down. It was perhaps just a coincidence that the Pavilion on the Low Green featured roller skating as an attraction that year. In 1930, on the site of the ill-fated former skating rink, a new Green's Playhouse was built which could seat over 3,100 and in years to come was to host concerts, both classical and pop, and other events, as well as showing films. Like many former cinemas, it is now a bingo hall.

Above: The roof of Wellington Chambers again provides the vantage point for this view along Fullarton Street to the Holy Trinity Episcopal Church and the Jarvis International Hotel. The church was built in 1898 as the major Scottish work of architects J.L. and F.L. Pearson; J.L. Pearson is best known for designing Truro Cathedral. The tower was not completed until 1964 and precast concrete was used. The site of Appleyard's Garage (formerly Fraser's garage) has since been taken by a car park, while part of Fullarton Street has been converted for westbound one-way traffic only.

Left: Although the Gaiety Theatre in Carrick Street looks as though a bomb has hit it, this picture was actually taken during a renovation scheme in 1995. Once enlarged and reopened, a new cafe and more facilities for artists and patrons were included. Popplewell's Cafe, on the new site, is named after the famous family who ran the theatre for nearly fifty years until it was threatened with closure and the town council took it over in 1974. The theatre was originally opened in 1902, although it had to be rebuilt the following year after a fire.

Opposite: The geometrical plan of Wellington Square, its gardens and the surrounding streets is remarkable when compared with the unplanned clutter of the mediaeval town at the top of the picture. The Sheriff Court and County Buildings are seen at the foot; the former was built between 1818 and 1822 and the County Buildings were added in 1931. From the Sandgate and High Street ports, the town swelled to the south in the nineteenth century and kept going throughout the twentieth; indeed, at Alloway and Doonfoot two miles to the south the expansion still continues, while the pressure to expand inland is only contained at present by the Ayr bypass.

Wellington Square dates back to the early years of the nineteenth century and owes its name to the popular hero of the time, the 1st Duke of Wellington, victor at Waterloo in 1815. The square looks quite empty in this view from the early 1900s with a total lack of landscaping; the railings were removed during the First World War for the war effort. The statue is of Archibald William, 13th Earl of Eglinton and Winton, and it was erected in 1865, four years after his death. The tall red sandstone building in the background left is Wellington Chambers which was built in 1895. The buildings further along on the east side of the square are typical early nineteenth century.

Wellington Square from the north-east corner in 1939. By this time the square had undergone quite a transformation. The garden had been landscaped and the two statues that were there already (including that of Brigadier James George Smith Neill which was not visible in the above picture) have been joined by that of Sir James Fergusson of Kilkerran, erected in 1910. In the far south-west corner is a less obvious memorial to John Loudon Macadam, the famous road-maker. Prominent in the centre is the cenotaph. To the west of the square is the Sheriff Court and County Buildings, which had been extended four years earlier, and in the distance the Low Green with the Pavilion just visible. Today, over sixty years on, little has changed in the garden, although a fairly recent addition is the Kennedy Memorial, a red granite obelisk and fountain, which previously stood at the junction of Fort Street and the Sandgate and commemorates Primrose William Kennedy, a banker and provost of Ayr.

Milrig Hotel, Ayr.
Tel. 901, - Proprietrix . Mrs. C. Roche.

Milrig House in Charlotte Street was built around 1805 for Major John Webster. For a time the Misses Baird ran a boarding school in it for young ladies and like a number of other large houses in the town it was later converted into a hotel. For many years in the early part of the twentieth century the hotel was owned by Mrs Roche. Advertising material of the time described the tennis court, putting green, summerhouse and gardens. On 1 April 1939 it was acquired by the town council for £6,355 for use as the burgh police headquarters. It later was used as the Burgh Civil Defence Headquarters, but by 1960 the building was derelict and considered an eyesore in a residential area. It was suggested that the council should develop the site for luxury flats or a first-class hotel, but in 1970 Milrig was demolished and more than thirty years later the site is still vacant and used as a car park. This view shows the rear of the building and the garden. Close to the house was the carpet factory of James Templeton & Son which was destroyed by a fire in 1876 with the loss of twenty-nine lives.

The Tower of St John is all that remains of Ayr's original parish church which was dedicated to St John the Baptist, the town's patron saint. The church dated from around the thirteenth century, although the tower was probably added in the fourteenth century. In 1654 Oliver Cromwell's army requisitioned the church as part of the Citadel and used it as an armoury with the tower becoming a lookout post. The Citadel was one of four forts Cromwell built in Scotland

during the troubles following the Civil War and was dismantled after the Restoration. The church ceased to be used for religious purposes some thirty years later and soon after was demolished, save for the tower. In time the former Citadel area came under the ownership of the Kennedys of Cassillis and in 1853 it was bought by John Miller, an Ayrshire-born gunsmith who made his fortune in Calcutta. A somewhat eccentric individual, Baron Miller (as he became known after he bought the lands of the Barony of Montgomeriestown) converted the Tower of St John into a Gothic-style residence which he called Fort Castle. After his death in 1910 at the age of eighty-nine, Fort Castle was purchased by the Marquis of Bute who removed the additions of Miller and restored the tower to its original character. He presented it to the burgh in 1914.

Montgomerie Terrace was originally known as Montgomeriestown Terrace, recognising the name of the barony which had been created in 1663 out of the fort area. The villas on the left are easily recognisable today, but the wild-looking area in the foreground has been occupied by tennis courts for over sixty years.

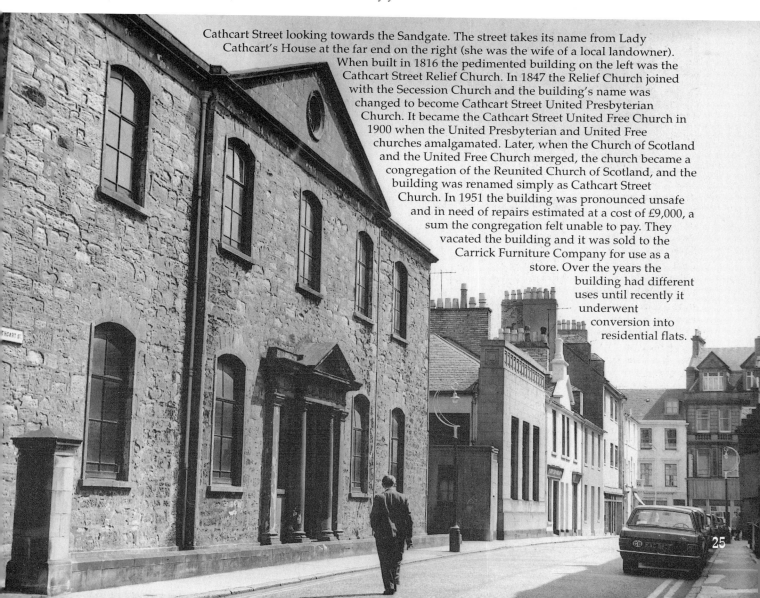

Cathcart Street looking towards the Sandgate. The street takes its name from Lady Cathcart's House at the far end on the right (she was the wife of a local landowner). When built in 1816 the pedimented building on the left was the Cathcart Street Relief Church. In 1847 the Relief Church joined with the Secession Church and the building's name was changed to become Cathcart Street United Presbyterian Church. It became the Cathcart Street United Free Church in 1900 when the United Presbyterian and United Free churches amalgamated. Later, when the Church of Scotland and the United Free Church merged, the church became a congregation of the Reunited Church of Scotland, and the building was renamed simply as Cathcart Street Church. In 1951 the building was pronounced unsafe and in need of repairs estimated at a cost of £9,000, a sum the congregation felt unable to pay. They vacated the building and it was sold to the Carrick Furniture Company for use as a store. Over the years the building had different uses until recently it underwent conversion into residential flats.

The New Parish Church was built between 1807 and 1810 to accommodate the overspill from the Old Parish Church (which was off High Street) when its congregation outgrew that building. In effect the Ayr Old and New churches were the first and second charges of the Old Parish Church of St John. In 1951 it was decided to unite the two charges, the new sole charge becoming known as the Auld Kirk of Ayr. The congregation of Cathcart Street Church, having had to vacate their premises, moved across the road to the New Church, and preserving their identity, became known as Cathcart Church. At the time it was stressed that there was no question of any union between the New Church and Cathcart. In 1981 the Cathcart congregation left with that of Sandgate Church to unite with Trinity Church, forming Ayr St Columba, and a few years later the redundant church premises were converted into the dance studio, Dansarena.

26   The interior of the Cathcart Church before its conversion into Dansarena.

In the past dancing in the kirk would have scandalised some of the town's citizens, but with the reopening of the redundant Cathcart Church in Fort Street as Dansarena, dancing, keep fit classes, music lessons and even a concert by the Scottish Baroque Ensemble have given new life to the building. Karen Mitchell is pictured leading a class of young dancers in one of the studios.

The first mention of the 'School of Ayr' was in 1233 when Pope Gregory IX appointed a commission to investigate a dispute over land. One of the members of the commission was described as *'magister scholarum de are'* ('schoolmaster of the scholars of Ayr'). It wasn't until the 1790s that the term 'Academy' was used and 1800 when a building on the present site was occupied.

This early 1900s view from the north shows the building of 1880 which still forms the front of the present school. Over the years the building expanded considerably with an Art Department (1907), Central Hall (1911–12) and Memorial Hall (1939) amongst the major constructions. Above the central entrance are three stone heads representing Literature, Art and Science, viz. Robert Burns, Sir David Wilkie and James Watt.

Ayr Academy pupils rehearse in the boys' gymnasium for their town hall performances of Gilbert and Sullivan's *Patience* in 1957. Music teacher William E. Glover is in charge along with producers Marion McWilliam and Kennedy Smith (respectively, they were affectionately known as Teddy, Pussy, and K.S.). Teddy Glover's contribution to the musical world of Ayr Academy was outstanding. Many troubled youngsters had their lives transformed and their attitudes to education improved by joining his lunchtime practices which led up to the annual G. and S. production. The gym teacher for many years was T.B. Watson.

AYR ACADEMY CHOIR

PRESENTS

GILBERT & SULLIVAN'S OPERA

"PATIENCE"

(By permission of Bridget D'Oyly Carte)

IN THE

Town Hall, Ayr

ON

Wed., Thurs., Fri. and Sat.
19th, 20th, 21st and 22nd June
1957

The PRODUCTION under the DIRECTION of MARION MacWILLIAM and KENNEDY SMITH

Musical Director	WILLIAM E. GLOVER
Stage Directors	R. POLLOCK McKELL, CHARLES SUMMERS
Make-Up	CHARLES SUMMERS
Wardrobe	MARGARET J. PHILP
Scenery	Scenery designed by PAMELA OWENS and MARGARET HYSLOP and painted in the Art Department under the supervision of Mr CHARLES SUMMERS
Scenic Construction	Classes V. and VI. Technical Pupils:— PIERRE ARNOLD, ROBERT BRYDEN, DONALD CASKIE, ROBERT CLARK, EDWARD DAVIDSON, JOHN DUNN, JOHN FINNIE, DAVID HISLOP, ROBERT HOLLAND, COLIN HOPE, THOMAS KENNEDY, JOHN McCLOY, ROBERT McCULLOCH, J. NORMAN McLEAN, COLIN MURRAY, IRVING RORRISON, SAM STEVENSON, D. MALCOLM TROUP, and Members of Staff of the Technical Subjects Department.
Costumes	B. J. SIMMONS & CO. LTD., LONDON
Secretary	GEORGE STRACHAN
Treasurer	GRACE B. BABINGTON
Advertising and Publicity Manager	J. STEWART BROWN

In 1840 the Glasgow, Paisley, Kilmarnock & Ayr Railway line reached Ayr, the town's station having been opened a year earlier, in August 1839, at North Harbour Street. At that time there was no intention of extending the line further south and the site was ideal for a station as the shopping and business centre was only a few minutes walk across the New Bridge and was convenient for passengers going on ships leaving the harbour. Later, however, extensions were made to Dalmellington and Girvan and a new station was opened at the Townhead in 1857 (this was replaced by a new station – the present one – on a site close by in 1886). The North Harbour site then took on a new use as a goods station, handling imports and exports from the harbour.

In 1899 a girder railway bridge set on masonry pillars (also pictured opposite) was built to link the North and South harbours and carry rolling stock over the River Ayr to and from the main line. Over the years this was used to carry fish from the market on the south side. The railway bridge became less useful as goods traffic increasingly concentrated at the North Harbour and it was closed by the early 1960s, thereafter becoming a popular, but dangerous, shortcut for pedestrians crossing the river. After being damaged by floods its days were numbered and it was eventually demolished in 1978. All that remains today are four sets of round pillars across the river.

A ship takes advantage of the high tide to manoeuvre at the Wet Dock in this view looking towards the harbour mouth from around 1960. Two aspects of the harbour trade are to be seen, with the fish market and fishing boats on the left (south) side and cargo boats and handling equipment on the right (north) side. The twin-funnelled dredger Carrick sits at the North Quay. She was built at Renfrew and entered service in 1938 at Ayr where she worked for the next thirty years before being sold for service in Palermo. She was finally broken up in 1984. She could dredge up to thirty-two feet below water level, the spoil from her dredging being contained on board until she steamed out into the Firth and released it through doors in the hull. The clanking of the buckets as she dredged the river and the belching of black smoke as she headed out to sea will remain in the memories of many Ayr folk. From 1954 two giant fifty ton capacity electric coaling cranes dominated the North Harbour. These hoisted coal wagons over the holds of vessels moored alongside the quay and tipped in their contents.

30 A Dunure fishing boat, pictured in 1975, returns to the South Quay as the *Baltic Sun* and pilot boat wait to head to sea from the entrance to the Wet Dock. To the left of the square pilot house and conical leading light stands a coal shipping hoist, which like the great crane is no longer to be seen here.

Opposite: Ayr claims to be the oldest port on the west coast of Scotland with records dating back to the early thirteenth century. By the twentieth century the harbour consisted essentially of quays with berths on either side of the river, these having been rebuilt at various times in the eighteenth century, a tidal wet dock on the north side built in the early 1870s, and a smaller slip dock on the south side dating from 1883. The North Harbour mainly handled coal and freight traffic, while on the south side of the river the fishing fleet was based and passenger steamers operated. Other cargoes handled over the years have been fertilisers, timber, scrap metals, and even whisky. This aerial view of Ayr docks dates back to c.1925. On the north side of the river is the Wet (tidal) Dock with a plethora of railway lines leading from it. Overlooking its entrance is the harbour office with pepper pot turret and pilot house. Towards the centre of the picture is the lighthouse which seems oddly far inland. It was built 1841 and the keeper's cottage was added nine years later. On the shore at the top of the picture is the fertiliser factory on Saltpans Road. On the south bank of the river is the harbour light pier and swing bridge.

A popular spot for young boys was always at the quayside watching the fishing boats unload. With any luck you could pick up an odd mackerel to throw at someone or else take home for tea.

31

From 1821 steamers linked Ayr with Glasgow, and the following year a clipper-built yacht also began a twice weekly service. This was replaced three years later by a steam vessel which made the trip twice weekly and also soon began summer pleasure cruises. Although the coming of the railway to Ayr in 1841 ended the direct steamer service to Glasgow, the town was becoming a popular holiday resort and pleasure cruises became increasingly popular. By the 1870s there were regular excursion trips to Glasgow and to other Clyde ports such as Greenock. One of the steamers which ran these routes from the harbour was the *Bonnie Doon* which began sailing in 1876; on account of its not-infrequent mechanical problems it rapidly earned the nickname 'Bonnie Breakdown'. Later, the Glasgow & South Western railway purchased the large seagoing paddle steamer *Juno* and, with the exception of the war years, she served Ayr until the end of the 1931 season. The Caledonian Railway Company's *Duchess of Montrose* also provided regular pleasure cruises during the same period. In the 1930s the turbine steamer *Duchess of Hamilton* made regular summer cruises for a time and from 1954 the paddle steamer *Caledonia* was in operation.

In the mid-1970s the paddle steamer *Waverley* arrived on the Ayr cruise scene. She is pictured below sailing from the harbour for an evening cruise around Holy Isle, flying a colourful display of flags to celebrate her return to sailing after a refit. Ayr became a home base for the ship in 1975 in order not to compete with Caledonian Macbrayne ships farther up the Clyde; this was because Calmac very generously donated her to the Paddle Steamer Preservation Society for £1. Built in 1947, and now the last seagoing paddle steamer in the world, she has given pleasure to many thousands since then who are too young to remember the busy cruising days on the Clyde of the past. Regular sailings are still made from Ayr to destinations such as Brodick, Campbeltown, Loch Fyne and Ailsa Craig.

The turbine steamer *Duchess of Hamilton* leaves the North Harbour for an afternoon cruise to Arran in 1965. Built on the Clyde by Harland & Wolff in 1932, she was a regular visitor to Ayr until she was withdrawn in 1970 and later scrapped at Troon. The covered fish market and taller ice factory are seen to the right on the South Quay where the fishing fleet harboured.

During the eighteenth and early nineteenth centuries a number of ships were built at yards in Ayr, but it wasn't until the early 1880s that the Trustees of Ayr Harbour constructed a new shipbuilding yard next to the recently built slip dock on the south side of the river. The yard was operated by Samuel MacKnight and Company and over the next eighteen years or so over sixty vessels were built, including a number of steamers, the largest being the *Lord Aberdeen* (1,360 tons) which was launched in 1889. In 1902 the six-berth yard was taken over by the recently formed Ailsa Shipbuilding Company of Troon (so-named because of the involvement of the Marquis of Ailsa). In the years until its closure in 1929

around two hundred vessels were built there, including coasters, steamers and barges. During the Second World War the yard reopened for repair work. The shipyard was acquired in 1947 by the Ayr Engineering and Construction Company (which had the Victoria Bridge Works), a subsidiary of the London Graving Dock Company, and they used it for repair work and some conversions of small vessels. The end of an era came with the closure of the yard, the site being sold to the town council by Associated British Ports in 1971 and the whole area being developed with blocks of flats. In the 1950s the slip dock, pictured here, was popular as a swimming and diving area.

The *Abraham Rydberg*, a four-masted barque, was an unusual visitor to the harbour around 1937 or 1938. A Swedish sail-training ship, she was pictured from the South Harbour. The rails in the foreground allowed goods traffic access to the South Harbour after crossing the rail bridge over the River Ayr.

As part of West of Scotland Water's new sewerage scheme for Ayr a 1,200 metre long storage tunnel for sewage and storm water was constructed, running under Ayr Harbour to a pumping station on the seafront at Newton. On completion of the tunnel (which had a 4.5 metre diameter) the public were allowed to walk through it from the North Harbour to an exit near Cromwell Road during a weekend in May 2000. Here a party is in the section under the south bank of the River Ayr, having just walked under the harbour.

There have been a few changes over the years in this section of South Harbour Street, not the least being the disappearance of the large seeds store in the foreground after a fire and subsequent demolition. Still watching over the street are the remains of a sentinel post on the old Citadel wall which in Victorian times was adapted as a gazebo by Baron Miller and has since become known as Miller's Folly. The building in the centre background, overlooking the street, is the Art Department building of Ayr Academy, erected in 1907.

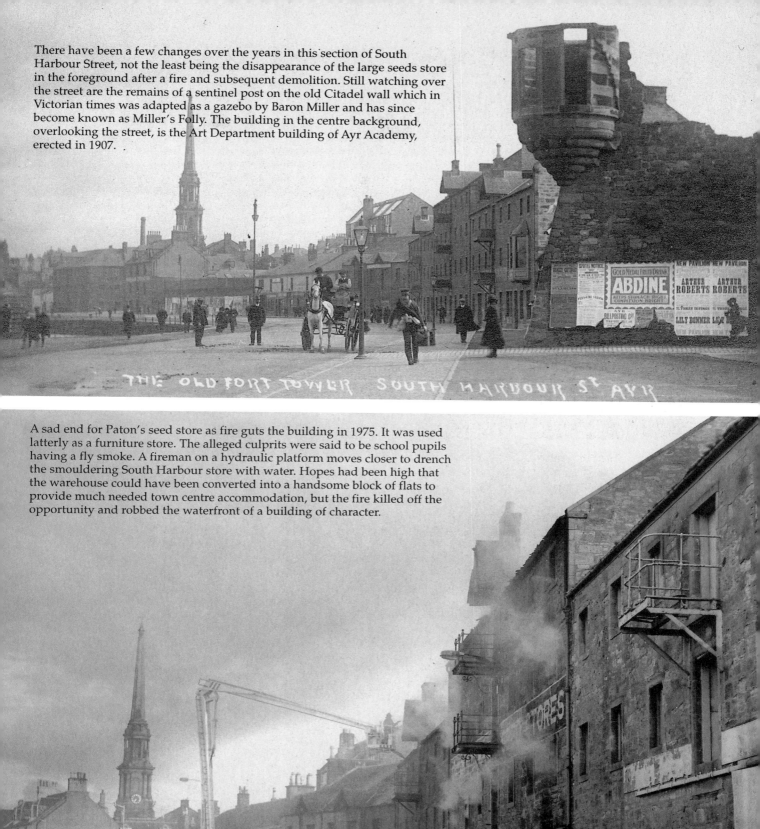

THE OLD FORT TOWER SOUTH HARBOUR St AYR

A sad end for Paton's seed store as fire guts the building in 1975. It was used latterly as a furniture store. The alleged culprits were said to be school pupils having a fly smoke. A fireman on a hydraulic platform moves closer to drench the smouldering South Harbour store with water. Hopes had been high that the warehouse could have been converted into a handsome block of flats to provide much needed town centre accommodation, but the fire killed off the opportunity and robbed the waterfront of a building of character.

Ayr Esplanade extends some two miles south from the harbour towards the mouth of the River Doon. The earliest development was in 1881 when the town council built a sea wall and promenade. Over the years this was added to, eventually being completed in 1925. In 1894 a local paper reported that 'the whole area for improvement was taken by the Burgh Surveyor from the esplanades at Gibraltar and other Mediterranean resorts, and its adaptation to the circumstances at Ayr promises to be a great success'. In more recent years South Ayrshire Council has been much concerned with modernising the appeal of the Low Green and the Esplanade, and has raised bitter opposition from those who consider some of the proposals as extravagant and wasteful of present assets. The 'Ayr Princess' on its miniature railway was a popular attraction for youngsters, running around a circular course, some times clockwise and sometimes anticlockwise to even out the wear on its wheel flanges. The baths and the walls of the Citadel can be seen in the background.

This aerial view puts into perspective the relative positions of some features described elsewhere in this book. The picture is dominated by the County Buildings and Courthouse with its domed roof, in front of which is Wellington Square. To the left of this, running towards the sea, is Bath Place with the bowling green opposite the side of the County Hotel. In the foreground the prominent houses are those of Queen's Terrace while the Steven Fountain is in the centre of the gardens in front of the County Buildings. The Pavilion stands out on the edge of the Low Green on the right.

The boating pond looking south towards the Low Green and Pavilion. This was situated close to the shipyard seen in the background of the picture of the play park below.

The sender of this postcard in August 1916 had 'just had a dip in the briny' and was 'having a fine day in this splendid looking place.' Everyone looks so overdressed for the beach – haven't times changed!

The writer of this postcard, called William, had 'spent a lovely day at [the] races' in September 1925. Remember struggling with these canvas and wooden deck-chairs that seemed to have a life of their own? The young chap on the left obviously hasn't the knack!

THE ESPLANADE, AYR.   288

A view from the mid-1930s, looking north along the Esplanade. Bathing chalets, which were rented out by the council on an annual basis, provided privacy for changing and also allowed storage of deck chairs, stoves and beach paraphernalia. These permanent structures are not to be confused with the bathing machines used much earlier in the century. Chalets were still on the beach into the 1950s, but were subject to vandalism and were eventually removed. Craigweil House is prominent on the right.

This happy group take to the water and join the children in this 1933 view with the Pavilion on the right and the then-recently extended County Buildings on the left. Funny to think that a few years earlier the town's prison occupied this latter site, affording its occupants tantalising views of freedom.

The fountain on the left – known as the Steven Fountain after James Steven who presented it to the town in 1892 – is of cast iron (not surprising as Steven was an ironfounder) decorated with dolphins and an otter with a fish in its mouth. Steven, whose business was in Glasgow, resided for a time at Skeldon House, near Dalrymple. The Pavilion – or the 'Piv' as it was known to many dancers in the 1950s and '60s, was built in 1911 at a cost of around £8,000 by the town council as an entertainment centre far the many summer visitors. At first it was commonly described as the 'white elephant on the Low Green'. It had seating for 1,500 people and over the years was used for dancing, roller skating, sporting events such as boxing matches, and summer variety shows. It was leased to Ben Popplewell (later Ben Popplewell & Sons) until 1967. Over the years its condition deteriorated and, while it continued to appeal to the youth of the town, it acquired some notoriety as a 'rave' venue under the name of Hanger 13. After sitting empty for several years it has recently undergone a refurbishment to become Pirate Pete's children's play centre. A feature of the main entrance was the balusters taken from the ruins of the 'old' New Bridge of Ayr after its collapse in 1877.

This photograph of the Bents was taken before the houses and indeed the road of Blackburn Drive were built, therefore dating it to around 1920 or slightly earlier, and looks west towards the Low Green from what is now a grassed area about half way along Blackburn Drive. The prominent villas in the picture are Carlton Turrets and Craigweil, both built in 1879 along with the nearby Westfield. Carlton Turrets was acquired in 1923 by Wellington School, which was then a private school for girls. Today it is co-educational and also occupies other property in the area. Craigweil was first occupied by George Coats of the Paisley thread family, before he took over Belleisle estate. Later, from 1932 until his death in 1960, it was owned by John C. Sword, the well-known transport pioneer. It became Ayr Youth Hostel in 1962.

The Low Green has always been a popular spot for Ayr residents and visitors alike. From the seventeenth century sports and games such as football and even croquet were played there. In recent years pipe band competitions have taken place on the green and it remains a place where crowds can gather for events or where children can play. However, it has never been far from controversy. Football matches were banned towards the end of the nineteenth century for fear of damaging the turf and proposals for sales booths came to nought over legal disputes. During the early years of the First World War the Royal Flying Corps used it as a landing strip (they went on to use the racecourse), and thirty years later Billy Butlin wished to acquire the land to build an amusement park. More recently plans have been produced to redevelop the whole area and these have not been met with widespread approval.

The bandstand on the Low Green dated back to Victorian times. On it the Burgh Band would play to delighted audiences each evening during the summer months. When this picture was taken in 1904 the bandmaster was Henry R. Sime. As the century proceeded the bandstand's popularity waned and its condition deteriorated until it was removed in 1952.

The road out of town leading to the bridge at Doonfoot was the Doonfoot Road. As the racecourse developed through the nineteenth century the section from the town to the racecourse became known, not surprisingly, as Racecourse Road. A narrow tree-lined thoroughfare, it has many large Victorian houses, some of which have been converted into hotels such as the Savoy Park, Gartferry, Pickwick, Old Racecourse and the Chestnuts, while others have become nursing homes. One of the earliest houses, Gargowan, is now part of the Ayrshire Hospice. At various times since the racecourse moved to its new site at Whitletts in 1907, two years before this photograph was taken, it has been suggested that the road's name should be altered to the more accurate 'Old Racecourse Road', but this has not been adopted.

In the late 1780s Hugh Hamilton of Pinmore acquired land which was once part of the Barony of Alloway and built on it a mansion which he named Belleisle, this being the name of a plantation he owned in Jamaica where he lived and made his fortune. His brother Robert bought and named Rozelle estate under similar circumstances. Belleisle remained in the ownership of other members of the Hamilton family well into the twentieth century, during which time the property was almost entirely reconstructed. A later owner was William Smith Dixon, a partner in the famous Glasgow ironmasters, Dixon and Company, during whose time the estate flourished. It then was bought by George Coats of the Paisley Thread

Company. While in the ownership of the Coats family the ballroom section of the house was added and wood carvings commissioned which depicted scenes from the works of Robert Burns. The estate, extending to almost 300 acres, was purchased by the town council in May 1926 at a cost of £25,000. Part of it was used to extend the existing golf course at the old racecourse to form the Seafield course, and partly to create the new Belleisle course (which at one time was considered to be among the finest public courses in Scotland); the remaining land was laid out as a public park. Over the years the park grounds around the golf courses were developed with a walled garden, walks, aviary, duck pond, pets corner and deer park. In Belleisle House a museum occupied the upper rooms for a time and Alexander Alexander displayed his collection of stuffed birds and animals. The house then became a hotel, much loved for its afternoon teas, and is now very popular for wedding receptions. There are few changes today from this early picture. Gone are the wall creepers and an extension has been added to the left of the building close to the steps.

Since this picture was taken in the early 1940s the conifers have grown considerably, there being some particularly fine specimens behind the rockery site. At the roundel intersection of the two central paths (extreme right) there is now a sundial which was presented to Belleisle by the National Association of Master Masons to commemorate their first National Conference to be held in Scotland in 1981. The prayer stone obelisk (so called because on its sides are biblical lessons for the seven days of the week) still stands next to the pond which is now sadly empty and neglected. In its heyday more than one curious youngster, anxious to see the goldfish, fell into it, and who can forget the wonderful display of the peacock strutting around just outside the walled garden?

47

This view of Belleisle's conservatory was taken in 1928, just two years after the council took over the estate. The conservatory was later rebuilt, reputedly around an established camellia, and many will fondly remember the colourful displays of pot plants on tiered benches, the bougainvilleas and abutilons, not to mention the observation beehive and the statue of a girl by W. Pfohl.

48   The topiary was a source of wonder and amusement for many years, but eventually it became too costly and time consuming to maintain. It fell into neglect and was removed around 1970.

Doonfoot Mill was situated on the south bank of the River Doon between its mouth and the bridge built in 1861 which takes the road out of Ayr. On account of the quantity of pearl barley produced, it became known as the barley mill. After its closure it was converted around 1896 into the Greenan Steam Laundry which was run for many years by the Bowie family. Its 100 foot chimney was a prominent feature in the landscape, but after the laundry closed it was demolished along with the buildings in 1971. This area of the river is popular for birdwatching and kingfishers can occasionally be seen hereabouts.

During the early years of the twentieth century territorial army units would hold annual camps at Doonfoot where they had a tough training programme. Judging by the number of bell tents here, it must have been quite a sight to see the men on exercise.

The massed layout of Wonderwest World, formerly Butlin's Holiday Camp, photographed in 1992. To some the central core of chalets, kitchens, restaurants and entertainment halls packed together might suggest more of a prison camp than a holiday camp, but this was a venue to which many thousands were willing to travel hundreds of miles for an annual vacation – at times using special train services.

Holidaymakers arrive at the Heads of Ayr Holiday Camp Station on a Saturday in June 1955. The station opened in May 1947 on the former Maidens & Dunure Light Railway, about a mile to the west of the original Heads of Ayr Station (on which a caravan park is now sited). This railway, which opened in 1906, was a single-track line which left the main Girvan line at Alloway Junction and ran to Dunure, Maidens and Turnberry before rejoining the main line near Girvan. It was known to railwaymen as the 'Shore Road'. The line was closed to passenger traffic in 1930 except for the Girvan to Turnberry section which served the Turnberry Hotel and survived until 1942. With the opening of Butlin's Holiday Camp, a section of the line was reopened with a new station for the camp. Trains arrived on Saturdays during summer months and came from all over the country. The station eventually closed in September 1968 and the track was lifted.

BUTLIN'S AYR
Miniature Railway & Boating Lake

For over forty years Butlin's Holiday Camp was the holiday venue for countless families who came to spend a summer fortnight in the chalets by the sea. It also provided casual employment for many local people. Just prior to the Second World War, Billy Butlin bought land at the Heads of Ayr and had his plans for a holiday camp and hotel well under way. However, with the onset of war a deal was done with the Admiralty whereby materials and labour were obtained to go ahead with the project and, once building was complete, the premises were left to the Admiralty for the duration of the war. It became a naval training establishment, HMS *Scotia*, with the hotel being the officers' quarters and the camp proper the ratings' accommodation and training area. In early June 1947 the holiday camp was finally opened by the wife of the head of the Scottish Tourist Board, who, in her opening speech to guests including Sir Harry Lauder, referred to 'the opportunity the camp provided the housewife to have a holiday free from domestic cares'. Initially it catered for 500 holidaymakers, but before long the numbers that could be accommodated rose to many times that figure. In 1988, after a number of changes, it was relaunched as Wonderwest World. However, ten years later the original camp was demolished and replaced by Craig Tara Park which contains static caravans rather than chalets.

One of the attractions of the Heads of Ayr Hotel.

It's
a pleasure
to dance
to -

THE PRINCESS BALLROOM ORCHESTRA

in the truly colourful setting of this magnificent Ballroom.

Soft Lights.   Sweet Music.   Inlaid floor of teak and African mahogany.
            Dancing for the Connoisseur.   Soda Fountain.

PRIVATE PARTIES AND DANCES ARRANGED.   SPACIOUS CAR PARK.

Special late buses leave for Ayr and Prestwick after the dances have ended.
Special public Holiday Dances will be held during the Summer Season and will be announced in the local press beforehand.

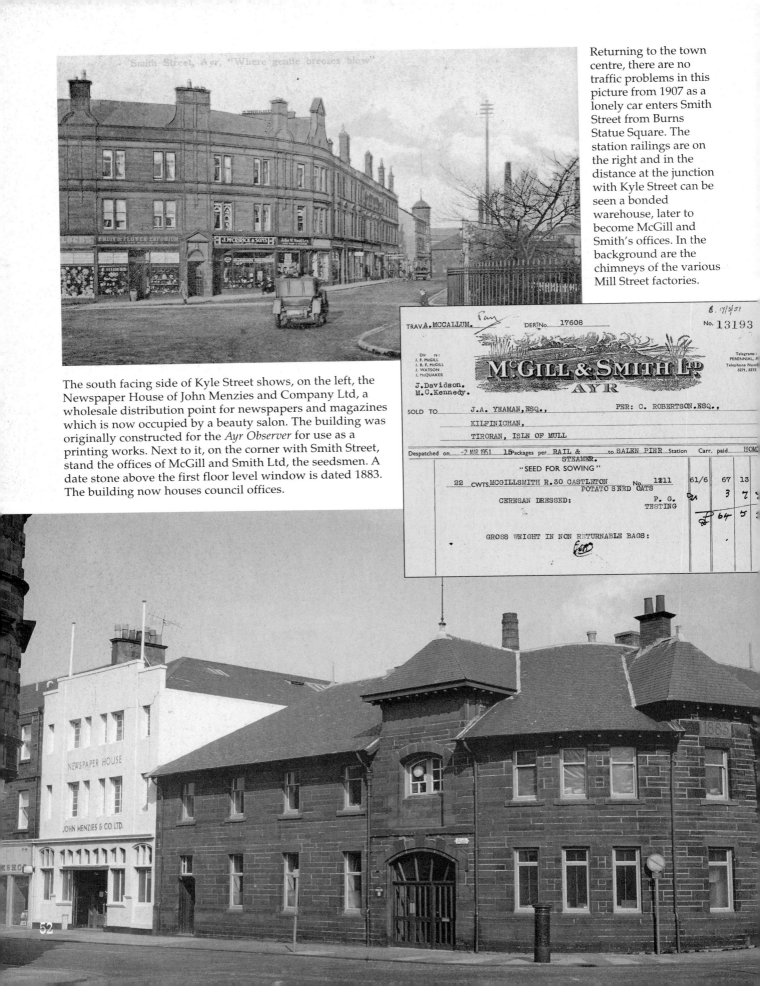

Smith Street, Ayr, "Where gentle breezes blow"

Returning to the town centre, there are no traffic problems in this picture from 1907 as a lonely car enters Smith Street from Burns Statue Square. The station railings are on the right and in the distance at the junction with Kyle Street can be seen a bonded warehouse, later to become McGill and Smith's offices. In the background are the chimneys of the various Mill Street factories.

The south facing side of Kyle Street shows, on the left, the Newspaper House of John Menzies and Company Ltd, a wholesale distribution point for newspapers and magazines which is now occupied by a beauty salon. The building was originally constructed for the *Ayr Observer* for use as a printing works. Next to it, on the corner with Smith Street, stand the offices of McGill and Smith Ltd, the seedsmen. A date stone above the first floor level window is dated 1883. The building now houses council offices.

Mill Street today is mainly a housing area and gives little hint of its industrial past. This photograph dates from around 1980 before redevelopment took place, with the nineteenth century tannery overlooked by the chimney of James Templeton and Company's worsted mill complex.

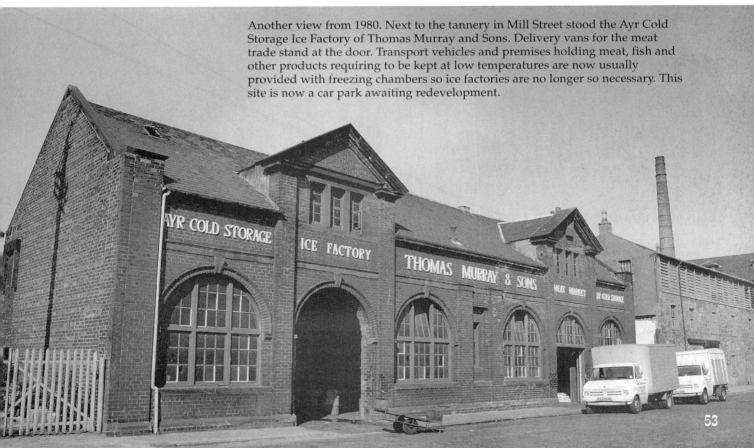

Another view from 1980. Next to the tannery in Mill Street stood the Ayr Cold Storage Ice Factory of Thomas Murray and Sons. Delivery vans for the meat trade stand at the door. Transport vehicles and premises holding meat, fish and other products requiring to be kept at low temperatures are now usually provided with freezing chambers so ice factories are no longer so necessary. This site is now a car park awaiting redevelopment.

Ayr Fire Station gives a fine view across the River Ayr between the Victoria Bridge and the Ayr Station and the Carrick Hills. Ayr No. 1 Signal Box, closed in 1985, guards the northern approach to the station; through lines to the south are on the left, while on the right are bay platforms for the Ayr–Glasgow service with D.M.U.s at platforms 2 and 4. The sidings on the right at Smith Street are now the site of a car park and flats. At the top left of the picture is the

now restored Holmston House which was once the Kyle Combination Poorhouse. This was built between 1857 and 1860 to accommodate 250 inmates and fifty lunatics from Ayr and neighbouring areas. The Market Inn to its right sits in front of the Cattle Market which is now the site of a Safeway supermarket. The factories at the bottom left of the picture have been replaced by a car park.

Pictured in 1975, men of Ayr Fire Station carefully check and pack breathing apparatus for the side-loading compartment of their Bedford fire engine. While there is evidence of the town having fire engines as far back as the eighteenth century, it wasn't until 1914 that the first motor fire engine was purchased, followed by two others in 1921 and 1927. The present station was built on the site of Content House which was built in the early 1800s and was for many years the home of the McIlraith family. It fell into disrepair and in the early 1950s it was occupied by squatters before being demolished in the early '60s. The fire station was opened in May 1963 by Daniel Sim, convenor of Ayr County Council, and William Cowan, the town's provost. Prior to this, the fire brigade had been based in the Sandgate on a site previously occupied by Mackie's garage.

Craigie House was built around 1730 for Sir Thomas Wallace on a knoll on the north bank of the river surrounded by trees. Later that century it became the property of the Campbell family and remained in their ownership for over 150 years until it was sold to the town council for £12,500 in 1939. During the war years it was requisitioned by the army and was used for a time as the headquarters for the Ayrshire Yeomanry, then still a cavalry regiment. After 1945 Craigie House was run as a tearoom and function centre and in the '50s the gardens were developed and walks created. In 1964 the house became part of the new Craigie College of Education, housing the music and drama departments.

The college later merged with the University of Paisley. Recently, it was refurbished to its former glory and became home of the Ayrshire Management Centre. The parts of the gardens close to the Dam Park were the site of the Parks Department's workshops and plant nursery. In the mid-1990s the nursery site was developed into the Craigie Horticultural Centre with display glasshouses, sales area and tearoom. A long-standing feature of the gardens is the Pansy – or, more correctly, viola – Walk, a continuous bed approximately a quarter of a mile long. Many apprentice gardeners have suffered over the years, planting and tending the bed of some 14,000 plants. Further along this riverside walk is Craigholm Bridge, a footbridge which links this area with the walk at Holmston on the south bank.

The River Ayr has frozen over in this view from the 1950s or '60s towards the Craigie Gardens, and the public have taken the rare opportunity to slide, skate and play ice hockey on it. After a few days the ice thinned and people were warned away, although some ignored the warning and managed to fall through it. They were lucky to survive.

Ayr County Hospital pictured from the Victoria Bridge which was originally built in 1898 and rebuilt in 1961. The weirs on the River Ayr stand opposite the site of the Nether Mills (barley mills which also produced snuff) which is now used as a car park. Salt water from the Firth of Clyde can reach up to the weirs at high tide.

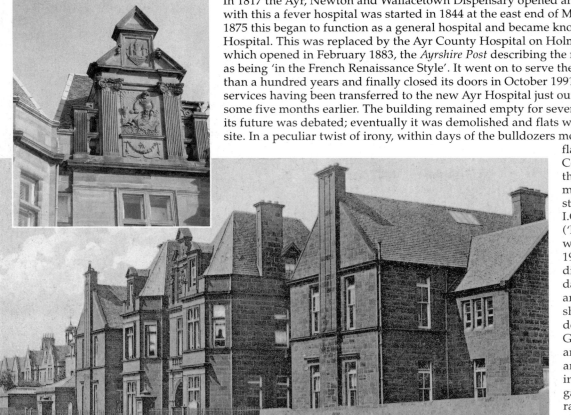

In 1817 the Ayr, Newton and Wallacetown Dispensary opened and in association with this a fever hospital was started in 1844 at the east end of Mill Street. In 1875 this began to function as a general hospital and became known as the Ayr Hospital. This was replaced by the Ayr County Hospital on Holmston Road which opened in February 1883, the *Ayrshire Post* describing the main building as being 'in the French Renaissance Style'. It went on to serve the town for more than a hundred years and finally closed its doors in October 1991, the outpatient services having been transferred to the new Ayr Hospital just outside of town some five months earlier. The building remained empty for several years while its future was debated; eventually it was demolished and flats were built on the site. In a peculiar twist of irony, within days of the bulldozers moving in to flatten 'the County', one of the best-known members of its staff, Miss Agnes I.C. Bone ('Nana'), who was matron from 1959 to 1970, died. This view dates from around 1908 and shows the front door with the Good Samaritan and burgh coat of arms above (see inset) and the gate in the railings on the right hand side which gave access to the dispensary.

Over the years a popular local walk has been the River Ayr Walk, created in 1910 and extending along the south bank of the river from opposite the cemetery entrance in Holmston Road to the Stepping Stones. Initially there were objections to the idea by local landowners Richard Oswald of Auchincruive and J.A. Campbell of Craigie, but happily they were resolved. It is possible to walk the north bank of the river from the harbour to the Stepping Stones upriver of Overmills Bridge (which carries the bypass over the river). The south bank has a few obstacles in the way from the harbour upstream, such as between the New and Auld Bridges, but it is a clear walk from opposite the cemetery gates on towards the Stepping Stones. The structure in the picture is the ruin of a limekiln which can still be seen along the walk, between Craigholm and Overmills Bridges. It dates from the mid-eighteenth century and was fuelled with coal from Holmston Pit. Close to the limekiln is 'Wallace's Heel', an imprint in a rock supposedly left by William Wallace after leaping across the river while being pursued by English soldiers.

A popular picnic spot by the River Ayr used to be at the Stepping Stones. Situated upriver of Overmills Bridge, which takes the A77 Ayr by-pass over the river, these large concrete blocks, which are still in place, allowed a crossing close to the Over Mill which was situated on the south bank.

The Over Mill, or Overmills, once one of fourteen mills on the River Ayr, was the last to survive, closing in 1945. The property of the burgh of Ayr, it had been in use for over 300 years and a mill had stood on this site since the thirteenth century. While it was essentially a corn mill, in the mid-eighteenth century a waulk mill was built on to it for the processing of cloth.

Auchincruive is synonymous the world over with the West of Scotland Agricultural College (now known, somewhat regrettably, as 'S.A.C. – Ayr Campus'). For over seventy years students from the college have gone on to hold positions in all aspects of agriculture and horticulture, including farming, managing, advising, teaching, and researching. Locally, as well as being a source of employment, the college was renowned for its fine gardens and its fruit, dairy and poultry produce. It is also known worldwide as the 'birthplace' of the strawberry varieties bred by Robert D. Reid between the 1940s and '60s, with names such as Auchincruive Climax, Talisman and Redgauntlet. Auchincruive House was built in 1767. It was enlarged in the late nineteenth century and the estate, having been in the Oswald family for many years, was purchased by John Hannah of Girvan Mains and gifted to the college in 1927. Later renamed Oswald Hall, it was for a long time the female students' hostel. It has recently undergone major refurbishment and is used as a conference and entertainment centre. This south facing view dates from 1935.

This view will arouse many memories of the gardens. The glasshouses in the foreground and distance were used for tomato production, while the range in between had peach houses, vineries and a plant house. In front of the lecture room (the building just beyond the nearest glasshouses) was a spectacular old wisteria and a fig tree, and more recently a magnolia. The herbaceous borders were magnificent and the yew hedges, reputedly planted around 1770, were almost as wide as they were tall. A bronze statue of Richard Oswald's bull terrier, Teddy, who died in 1872 aged sixteen, is just visible to the centre-right of the picture. Inevitably over the years there have been many changes. The east and west range glasshouses were demolished in 1982, the yew hedges removed many years ago, and Teddy was stolen.

Little is known about this suspension bridge which is believed to have crossed the River Ayr in the wood beyond the head gardener's house. The postcard is dated July 1914, but it is thought that the bridge did not survive very much longer.

The sheep ring at the old livestock market of James Craig Ltd near the station roundabout. In 1890 the Cattle Market moved from the top of Alloway Street (just north of Burns Statue Square) to the site across the railway where Safeway supermarket stands today. In 1993 it moved to an out-of-town site on the Ayr–Cumnock road. The white-coated auctioneer is Alex Andrew, the co-author's father, who worked for Craig's for forty-nine years before his retiral in 1966.

Opposite: Parkhouse Street and the massive bulk of the Ayr Ice Rink, pictured from the roof of the Station Hotel. When it opened in March 1939 the rink was the largest and most up-to-date in Scotland and cost in the region of £90,000 to build and equip. It was built on what was formerly part of Beresford Park, one-time ground of Ayr Parkhouse F.C. Over 1,000 skaters could be accommodated on the rink's 20,000 square feet. After closure as an ice rink in 1974 the building was converted into a Safeway supermarket and has remained empty since this moved to the present site across the railway. The car park on the right, with the white-coated attendant, was for patrons of the Odeon cinema which is behind it. The council offices of Burns House now stand on the site of the car park. McQuiston no longer owns the garage, although it is still a filling station.

Above: Sweepers from the Nithsdale Ladies Club guide a curling stone to the centre circle in the ice rink. The rink was big enough to also accommodate skaters on the ice around curling matches in progress. A new and smaller ice rink at Tam's Brig replaced the old rink in 1974 and this itself was replaced by the Centrum Arena.

The photograph on the left shows an exhibition ice hockey match between Brighton Tigers and Paisley Pirates, played on 11 February 1959. In the 1950s capacity crowds of over 4,000 often turned up at the ice rink on a Friday night to cheer on Ayr Raiders, a team formed after the Second World War, and the sport became very popular locally. The team consisted almost entirely of Canadian players (a situation which continues to this day with Ayr Scottish Eagles). When the ice rink closed in 1974 the sport moved to the new rink at Tam's Brig and the team became known as Ayr Bruins. They later played for a short time at the Summit Centre in Glasgow. After a gap of several years ice hockey returned to the area in the mid-1990s with the opening of the Centrum Arena in Prestwick and the team became known as Ayr Scottish Eagles.

Carrick House Auxiliary Hospital was one of two such Red Cross establishments in Ayr during the First World War, the other being Seafield House. Carrick House was lent to the Red Cross by Mrs Elizabeth Arthur, widow of Thomas Glen Arthur, a prominent Glasgow businessman and merchant who died in Algeria in 1907. Situated off Carrick Road between Carrick Avenue and Broomfield Road, the house was built around 1844 as a plain Victorian two storey and basement mansion, although over the years various alterations were made. This view, from around 1917, shows the back of the house facing the garden and the first floor veranda. The message on the reverse of the card is dated 6 September 1917. The hospital was opened on 9 November 1914 and by 1918 had 100 beds and had treated well over 2,000 patients. During part of this time the surgeon there was Dr James S. Geikie who became well known at the County Hospital for the following thirty years or so. Patients treated at the Auxiliary Hospital also included foreign allies, some of the first contingent being Belgian. Eventually the building fell into disrepair and neglect. In 1976 plans to demolish the house, lodge and outhouses and replace them with twenty-eight flats met with opposition, particularly from the local Civic Society who claimed that the house contributed to the character of the area, 'taking its place as one of the substantial houses which formed the original development of the area and not deserving to be wiped off the face of the area'. After a temporary reprieve the pleas were rejected and Carrick House was demolished in the early 1980s. The site was subsequently developed as superior wardened housing and became known as Carrick Gardens.

Rozelle Estate, inland from Belleisle on the road to Alloway, was formed on common land sold by the town council to Robert Hamilton in 1754. Hamilton, who had made his money in Jamaica, gave it the name of Rochelle after a property of his there (over time the name became Rozelle). His mansion was built in 1760 and was later enlarged according to plans by David Bryce in 1830 when the house was still in the Hamilton family. In 1968 the then-owner, Lieutenant Commander J. Hamilton RN, presented the house and estate to the town for cultural and recreational purposes. In the picture the house is seen from the pond-walk and nature trail which opened in 1970 as a contribution to European Conservation Year.

Opposite: Bill McEwen sent this postcard in February 1910 to his younger brother James in Washington DC with the message, 'This is the garage where I am Time Keeper & Storeman'. When this picture was taken the Ayr County Motor Co. had recently moved from 74 Dalblair Road to new premises at 15 Beresford Terrace, the Dalblair Road garage being subsequently occupied by Cocker & Ross. Another garage in town at that time was Hugh McQuiston of Beresford Lane. In this view of part of their spacious premises, a Rolls–Royce 40/50 h.p. 'Silver Ghost', registration R 534, can be seen in the right foreground. It was acquired by the Marquis of Bute in August 1908 and later belonged to John C. Sword who was an avid collector of veteran and vintage cars.

In this view looking towards Ayr, a tram travelling on the Burns Monument route is making its way through Rozelle Woods, passing Meikle Stane Cottage which is long since gone. This route from St Leonard's Church to the Burns Monument Hotel, which passed through woodland and countryside, must have been one of the most scenic town tramway journeys in the country. The Ayr Corporation Tramways system officially opened in 1901, operating between Prestwick Cross and St Leonard's Church. In June 1902 the line was extended an additional two miles from St Leonard's Church to Burns Monument.

Below: Formerly known as Greenfield, the estate of Cambusdoon was purchased in 1853 by James Baird of the famous family of iron and coal masters, and he built a mansion house on it. In 1926 Ayr Preparatory School, having already occupied several different premises in the town, moved to Cambusdoon, and renamed as Cambusdoon School for Boys, remained there until its closure in 1967. Several years later the building was demolished. Little remains today, notably a ruined archway off Shanter Way. Baird's name is remembered in Baird Road, close by in Alloway. This view of the house dates from 1904.

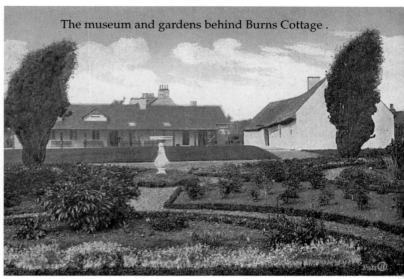

The museum and gardens behind Burns Cottage.

Few poets' birthplaces can be as well known as that of Robert Burns. Throughout the world the image of Burns Cottage at Alloway is immediately recognised. In 1759 Burns was born in the cottage, which had been built by his father two years previously, and lived there for the first seven years of his life. A few days after the poet's birth storm damage caused the building to partly collapse, but his father, William Burnes, rebuilt it well enough for it to have remained intact ever since. It was after Burns's death that the cottage became something of a Mecca to his enthusiasts. The Burns family had sold it in 1781 to the Incorporation of Shoemakers who ran it as a public house, and 100 years later it was acquired by the Trustees of the Burns Monument who restored it to how it may have looked in the poet's time. In 1900 a museum was built adjoining the cottage and this remains one of Scotland's most popular tourist attractions.

Burns Bi-centenary Celebrations

The Burns Federation and
Ayr Town Council

present

Andrew Keir

in

"I, ROBERT BURNS"

A Pageant

with ANNETTE CROSBIE, EILEEN PRICE, GWYNETH GUTHRIE and
CHARLES GREVILLE

in GREEN'S PLAYHOUSE, AYR, 16th – 20th JUNE, 1959
Overture, 7.30 p.m.

To mark Burns's Bicentenary the Burns Federation and Ayr Town Council presented a pageant in the Green's Playhouse in June 1959, entitled *I, Robert Burns*. The cast included Andrew Keir in the title role, Annette Crosbie as Jean Armour and Gwyneth Guthrie as Mary Campbell. It featured many local actors and musicians and even one of this book's authors had a small non-speaking, walk-on/walk-off part! The music was composed and arranged by Ian White, founder and conductor of the BBC Scottish Orchestra who had studied composition under Vaughan Williams, and the orchestra had many fine local players including a cellist who went on to achieve international fame as a conductor, Bryden (Jack) Thomson.

A group of rather benign looking witches chase Tam o' Shanter and his mare Meg up the Auld Brig o' Doon, albeit at a rather more leisurely pace than that described in the poem. The Tam o' Shanter Ride was an annual event for a number of years from about 1970, but was later discontinued. Tam was played by James Armstrong, while the young ladies were student teachers from Craigie College of Education.

BURNS MONUMENT AND HOTEL, AYR.

The Banks o' Doon Tea Gardens were situated on the northern bank of the Doon between the old and new bridges. The gardens were developed from a neglected apple orchard. For a charge of 2*d*. for an adult and 1*d*. for children, visitors could stroll through the gardens, which were resplendent with climbing roses and other flowering shrubs, and on evenings and weekends from April to October listen to music played by various groups of musicians. During the twenties the Tramways offered special return fares to the monument on concert nights at the Tea Gardens. Refreshments could be had within the bungalow where there was a collection of historical relics and pictures, while souvenirs could be purchased in the shell grotto. The lower picture with Burns Monument on the right includes the new Bridge of Doon (built in 1816), beyond which can be seen the ornate railway bridge which carried the Maidens & Dunure Light Railway out of Alloway, having just passed through a tunnel under the Auld Kirkyard.

Opposite: Burns Monument was built in the early 1820s on a site overlooking the old and new bridges over the River Doon. The architect, Thomas Hamilton, also designed the Ayr Town Buildings. The nine columns of the temple represent the nine muses, while the triangular base represents and faces the three Ayrshire districts of Kyle, Carrick and Cunninghame. The nearby Burns Monument Hotel owes its origin to providing refreshments and accommodation for visitors to the monument. It was built eight years after the monument, adjacent to the new bridge. Once Ayr Corporation Tramways extended their line to the monument, Burns enthusiasts could retrace the ride of Tam o' Shanter all the way from the High Street inn, past Kirk Alloway, to the River Doon. The front of the hotel was the tram terminus. Today the monument remains a popular tourist attraction, while the hotel has undergone major refurbishment to become the Brig o' Doon House.

Right: A busy view of the Banks o' Doon Tea Gardens.

Auchendrane was formerly known as Blairston. David Cathcart was a prominent legal figure in the late eighteenth and early nineteenth centuries who, having been a judge, went on to become a Lord of Justiciary, taking the title Lord Alloway. Born in Ayr, he had inherited Greenfield (later Cambusdoon) before marrying Mary Mure, daughter of Dr Robert Mure of Blairston. She inherited Blairston in 1801, but she died the following year and the estate fell to Cathcart. The house remained in the Cathcart Family until the early part of the twentieth century. It was used as a nursing home until the 1990s, and is now empty.

Early in the twentieth century Longhill Avenue was a tree-lined country lane linking the Culroy Road near to the Bridge of Doon with the Dunure Road at Doonfoot. Legend has it that there was once a leper colony in the vicinity and that its last resident was one 'Kate'. Thus 'Kate's Avenue' became a popular name for the road. In later years the Glen Tea Gardens (below) was a popular refreshment stop as were a number of others in the Alloway area including, of course, the Banks o' Doon Tea Gardens and Mrs McNicol's Tearooms on Mains Hill. In 1962 many trees were felled amid public protest. Today the avenue and surrounding area has become a popular residential district of Alloway.

The Auld Brig pictured from its rival, the New Bridge, in 1907.

The Auld Brig has Robert Burns to thank for its continued existence today. Were it not for the fame bestowed upon it as one of the subjects of his poem 'The Brigs of Ayr' it probably wouldn't have survived the eighteenth century and almost certainly not the twentieth. There is reference from the thirteenth century to a bridge across the river, and over the centuries there were many reports of damage and decay and to repairs and sections rebuilt. Throughout the eighteenth century constant repairs had to be made until in 1782 an Act was passed empowering the town to build a new bridge joining the Sandgate with the Main Street of Newton. After this was built the Auld Brig was retained for pedestrian traffic only, but its problems continued and towards the end of the nineteenth century the council appeared reluctant to carry out any more repairs. There were suggestions that it be demolished; Sir William Arrol, designer of the Forth Bridge, felt that it was not worth preserving and should be removed. Many, however, felt it should be retained because of its historic and poetic connections, and the necessary money required to restore it was raised by public subscription. The restored bridge was reopened in July 1910 and is one of the oldest surviving stone bridges in Scotland.

Looking south over the Auld Brig from River Street around 1903. The building on the left still stands, having gone through a number of uses including sale room, tearoom and restaurant, but the shops next to it have long since disappeared.

A wintry scene to the north of the Auld Brig with slushy roads, frozen pavements, and cobbles that were no doubt hazardous to anyone venturing out that night. River Street, on the left, and Wallace and George streets were all through roads at this time. The Black Bull is seen on the left with 'the Children's Corner' and Robertson's the electricians next door. The shops, Gospel Hall, and Wallace Street were all swept away for the development of a Gateway supermarket (now an Asda). At one time a 'port' at this point on the bridge controlled entry to the burgh so that vagabonds and undesirables might be refused passage over the bridge and into the town.

The Auld Brig and Town Steeple are unchanging features in Ayr's townscape, although the buildings around them have changed considerably. Very few towns have pawnbroking offices now. This building was demolished to make way for a new Marks & Spencer store to replace the earlier premises which can just be seen on the right.

The New Bridge was completed in 1788, but had already featured in Burns's poem which had been written during its construction and was published the year before it opened. In it the Auld Brig boasts to its neighbour 'I'll be a brig when you're a shapeless cairn!', a prophesy which came true in 1877 when the south arch of the New Bridge suffered severe flood damage. The whole structure collapsed and had to be replaced by another (the present) New Bridge, built on the same site.

Looking towards the harbour around 1908, a tram crosses the New Bridge. On the right is the Darlington Place United Presbyterian Church (later known simply as Darlington New Church), while further along North Harbour Street is the goods station (the original Ayr passenger station).

A pre-1914 view looking north over the New Bridge with the Carnegie Public Library prominent on the left.

Looking downriver from the Fire Station in 1969. The tall Bison crane, echoed by a high crane at the harbour, is steadily adding concrete panels clad in marble and flint to one of three multi-storey blocks of flats rising north of the River Ayr. The tower blocks of fourteen storeys each were the only ones to be built in South Ayrshire. At that time Turner's bridge led left to open space at Mill Street, prior to new dwellings arising there. Scaffolding surrounds the town steeple which was in need of repair at the time.

A multi-storey block of flats gives a high viewpoint over Turner's Bridge in this view from 1969. The five arch steel footbridge was presented to the town in 1900 by A.M. Turner, a local brewery owner, and was lit by electricity from that time. A new suite of halls for the Auld Kirk's congregation stands by the river on the right with the Auld Kirk behind. The aged properties left of the halls have now been replaced by flats spanning over the Blackfriars Walk, which leads to the Wallace Tower and the High street.

The former Darlington Church is now used as the headquarters of the Borderline Theatre Company. Built as the Darlington Place United Presbyterian Church in 1860, it was known as Darlington New Church from 1948. It held its last service in 1981 when the congregation united with that of the Auld Kirk. The cross in the foreground of this early twentieth century view of the corner of Main Street and North Harbour Street is the Newton Mercat Cross, which was originally sited in the middle of Main Street in front of the Newton Steeple. River Street, from which this picture was taken, is today separated from the main road by a pavement and small garden area, save for access to what is essentially a parking area.

The Carnegie Library has featured greatly in the lives of the people of Ayr since it opened in September 1893, having been built at a total cost of nearly £12,000, paid for through the munificence of Mr Andrew Carnegie who offered the town £10,000 to build a free library on condition that the ratepayers adopted the Free Libraries Act. The librarian at the time lived rent free on the premises with free coal and gas. A guide for 1904, the year this postcard was sent, provided the opening times: 'Lending & Reference Departments, daily (except Wednesday): 1–4 p.m. & 6–9 p.m.; Wednesday: 10 a.m.–1 p.m.; Ladies Reading Room: daily, 9 a.m.–9.30 p.m.; General Reading Room: daily, 9 a.m.–10 p.m.' What would the unions and council think of these hours today? Generations of townsfolk have climbed up the steps, through the doors which do not seem to have ever altered, in their early years going to the children's library, then later progressing to the adult's. Also on the ground floor was the reference department and the reading room where people could read the newspapers and get a heat on a cold day. A further climb upstairs (past the impressive stained-glass window with the barefooted lady with six toes on one foot) led to the local museum where many children learned much about their town's history. Next door to the library, the Campbeltown Wine and Spirit Bar is still open for business, while on the other side of the library the name of Walter Mitchell & Sons, Bacon Curers, can still be seen in the upper front of the building, although their shop has long since gone to be replaced by the premises of a lighting shop and a butcher's.

For well over a century the name of Walter Mitchell was synonymous with bacon to the people of Ayr. It was in 1848 that the business began and after several changes of premises it arrived in 1870 at the site in Main Street where it was to remain for the rest of its illustrious life. The major part of the business was always bacon curing. By the end of the nineteenth century the firm was the largest curer of Ayrshire bacon in Scotland. As the firm grew depots were established in Glasgow, London, Liverpool and Manchester, and it became a major employer in the town. Changes in legislation after the Second World War meant that it became necessary for pigs to be killed in slaughterhouses (and not on farms), prior to be taken to factories for processing. Initially the firm's own staff operated at the burgh slaughterhouse, but in 1953 the company

opened its own slaughterhouse behind the Main Street premises. In the 1970s a major fire caused considerable damage and not long afterwards the firm closed down. The factory was demolished in 1979 and the site cleared. Sited at the corner of Garden Street and King Street, the 130 foot chimney could not be bought down by explosives for fear of affecting nearby roads and buildings, so it was left to a two-man team of steeplejacks to demolish it brick by brick. The factory site has now been taken by the flats of Garden Court.

A fireman tackles the blaze at Mitchell's from a position in Garden Street.

While awaiting redevelopment, the site of the Newton Church and Council Chambers became a car park and weekly open-air market, attracting traders from afar and many local shoppers. At one time a notice appeared identifying this as the site for Ayr Baths, but they were eventually built at the South Harbour. The Steeple and the Orient Cinema (shown screening *The Sound of Music*) still stand, although the cinema is now a nightclub. The market area is now occupied by the police headquarters which previously had stood in Charlotte Street. The Newton Steeple, built in 1795, was part of the Newton Town House and Tolbooth. The pend through the tower provided access to the old parish church of Newton, the gable of which can just be seen in the picture on the left which dates from around 1910. The town house and old church were demolished in 1967 to make way for a new road system.

The steel framework of the new police headquarters rises like a skeleton while concrete panels are hauled into place to be decorated later with brickwork. The building was opened in 1975.

A wintry day in King Street in 1970 with the Olympic Bar undergoing demolition at the corner of George Street. At that time vehicles could reach the town centre by driving through George Street to River Street, but George Street has since become a cul-de-sac.

A statue, erected in 1850, of Dr John Taylor stands on its high plinth in Wallacetown Cemetery at King Street, above the lower headstones, obelisks and urns. He was a prominent chartist in the nineteenth century and was much respected for his work on behalf of the underprivileged. The Ayr–Glasgow railway line runs in a cutting behind the statue. The Hawkhill Junction signal box, in the centre of the picture, formerly controlled the section between Newton-on-Ayr and the Ayr viaduct on the north approach to Ayr Station, but was destroyed by fire in 1970.

Opposite: Looking north along Main Street from the roof of the Carnegie Library. A Belisha beacon crossing leads to the door of the Orient Cinema which opened in 1932, and farther along the same side a shop is occupied by Ayr United Development Club. A Co-operative Drapery and Furniture Store can be seen to the right of the Newton gas holder which came into operation in 1956, having taken three years to construct. The height of this when fully distended was 167 feet, making it Ayr's second tallest structure after the town hall steeple. It was able to store over a million cubic feet of gas. At that time Ayr's gas system consisted of two distinct piping networks covering the northern and the southern parts of the town – a legacy of pre-nationalisation when they were two separate companies with gasometers at Damside and Cromwell Road. The origins of the Co-op in Ayr go back to 1896 when the Kilmarnock Equitable Co-operative Society (itself established in 1860) decided to open a branch in the town. The first grocery shop was in North Harbour Street, followed by one in Allison Street, and then a fleshing branch in Main Street. The success of these resulted in large new premises being built in New Road with a grocery and butcher's on the ground floor and a hall above. A bakery was established in McCall's Avenue in 1908. Later in Main Street a complex of Co-op stores were formed which included a pharmacy and a funeral service office. In 1984 the Co-op closed the last of its remaining shops in Main Street, leaving only the funeral service office which is still in business.

A view of Main Street from the Orient Cinema, 1969. The old church hall on the right has since been replaced and a new entrance made to the Newton Church behind. The tower of St James's Church rises above the council offices based in the former Unionist Club at the junction with Weaver Street, while the tall chimneys have since disappeared from the skyline.

This delivery van of David Paterson & Son, grocers and wine merchants, is typical of the 1930s.

This tram would pass Paterson's shop on its journey along Main Street between Prestwick Cross and Burns Monument. The picture dates from around 1915. During the First World War when shelling was feared from German submarines in the Firth of Clyde, a partial blackout was enforced and the trams' curtains were closed on the seaward side to block the bright lights of the upper deck.

The Trades Hotel, known as 'the Model', was a lodging house in York Street north of the harbour and offered cheap overnight accommodation to itinerant workers and the homeless. It is pictured after suffering a serious fire in 1969 which led to the building being demolished and the site redeveloped.

The sender of this postcard, written in November 1906, wrote 'I suppose you will manage to make me out.' Does anyone recognise D. Whyte in this picture, taken outside the Salvation Army's Citadel in New Road which opened the previous year? The Salvation Army Ayr Citadel Corps was established in 1896, but it was another nine years before new premises were built for them. The band was a familiar sight in Ayr on Sundays and today it continues to provide Christmas cheer in the High Street each December.

This view of New Road, from the gusset with Allison Street looking towards Tam's Brig, dates from the early 1900s. Most of the buildings are still identifiable, particularly the row of cottages on the right, although just beyond it, on the near side of the railway line, are premises formerly used as the Ebenezer Hall and also a shop. On the left some changes have taken place over the years. The first building has recently undergone tasteful alterations to the front and considerable development inside and to the rear to form a modern doctors' surgery. The frontage of the next block was altered and extended outwards many years ago, forming shops and the Vesta Cafe. In the next block is Tam's Brig Post Office, run for many years by Jim Hannah and his mother and grandmother before him. (In fact the same family ran it for over ninety years). The dominant structure in the right background is the Newton Junction signal box which closed in April 1965 and was subsequently demolished. At one time there were nine around the town's railway network, although none remain. The most striking difference today from this scene is the volume of traffic.

A steam locomotive joins the main line from the Harbour Branch at Newton-on-Ayr Station. This branch has been much used in the past for the export of coal. The tall chimneys are part of the Scottish Agricultural Industries factory and depot at Newton shore.

Left: In this smoky scene from the 1960s a class 4 standard British Rail locomotive, no. 76096, awaits an overhaul within Ayr motive power depot, situated beside the main line between Ayr and Newton-on-Ayr stations. The six-road stone-built shed (No. 67C) had a sizeable allocation of motive power, both passenger and goods, the latter for working the coal traffic of the Ayrshire coalfields. In December 1966 the shed closed as a steam depot. The more modern building which replaced it was used as D.M.U. sheds, but now part of it houses a wagon overhaul and maintenance unit and a smaller part is for locomotive maintenance.

A D.M.U. heads past the Falkland Yard north of Newton-on-Ayr on a wintry day. In the 1980s electrification of the line made the signal box and semaphore signals redundant. In the background is the huge Newton-on-Ayr gasometer and the Scottish Agricultural Industries factory.

Left: Engine no. 17384 approaching Newton Junction with a string of wagons from Ayr Dock in August 1939. At one time the harbour handled a lot of rail traffic in its numerous sidings, with coal the principal commodity being exported. In the background are the factories of Limekiln Road.

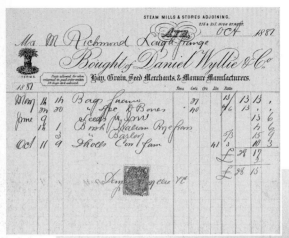

In 1860, on the site of the former Miller's factory at Newton Shore, A. Weir & Co. established the first factory in the west of Scotland for the production of super-phosphate for use as artificial fertiliser. Weir's firm was absorbed in 1880 by Daniel Wyllie & Co., which in turn became part of Scottish Agricultural Industries in 1928. To many older inhabitants of Ayr it is still known as Danny Wyllie's after its former owner. The palls of smoke from the factory were a familiar sight in the area, as were tankers delivering sulphuric acid to the plant and lorries leaving with sacks of fertilisers. The Scottish Agricultural Industries factory is seen across the Harbour Branch Railway at Newton-on-Ayr. The buildings in the foreground were designed by the office of Sir Basil Spence, architect of Coventry Cathedral.

Low tide at Newton exposes the ruins of heavy timber work and a large stone ring which is believed to have once been part of a coal pit or shaft. This is covered at high tide now but could have been farther back from the sea in the eighteenth century when coal was worked. Salt pans also existed in the area and the name Saltpans Road is a reminder of this industry today.

Trams making their way between Prestwick and Ayr along Prestwick Road, the main route into Ayr from the north, passing their depot – the 'car sheds' – situated on the right hand side, midway along the road. To the right is McCall's Avenue where various factories were situated including the Newton Carpet Works and the St Crispin Works which manufactured boots and shoes, specialising in heavy footwear for miners. The prominent square tower on the left is that of St James's Church, situated at the junction with Falkland Park Road. It originated as a separate North Newton congregation of Newton Parish Church in 1885, but was disjoined from Newton in 1904. This view is from Tam's Brig which crosses the main Glasgow–Ayr railway line. It was built around 1850 and was supposedly named after Thomas McCreath, a local worthy and farmer of Bellesleyhill which was nearby. Ayr

Prestwick Road, Ayr.

Corporation Tramways officially opened on 26 September 1901. Initially, in their chocolate and primrose livery, they ran between Prestwick Cross and St Leonard's Church, however in 1902 the line was extended to Burns Monument and in 1913 a branch line opened from the New Bridge to Hawkhill and the Racecourse. Thus, as well as carrying workers and shoppers to and fro, they catered for visitors going to Burns Cottage and beyond, as well as sports fans going to the races or Ayr United's ground, Somerset Park. The tram depot was known as Newton Park and was situated on Prestwick Road at the Bellesleyhill Road junction. The early sheds were on the south of Bellesleyhill Road and in 1923 an additional depot was built to the north of it. Many years after their closure the premises are still referred to by locals as the 'Car Sheds'. One shed is now a furniture showroom and filling station, while the other houses a discount supermarket.

This picture shows the interior of the original shed, probably around 1901–02, with car no. 3 prominent. This was a double deck open top, with seating for twenty-two inside and thirty-five on top.

Car no. 18 is seen here suitably decorated for the Coronation of 1911. This exhibition car, used only for special occasions, was sumptuously fitted out in the lower saloon and had stained leaded glass surrounds to the saloon windows.

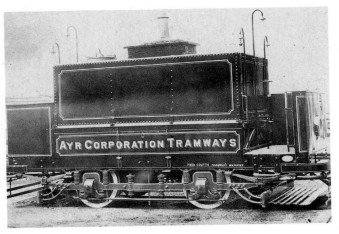

Car no. 17, a water sprinkler, had a tank of 2,240 gallons capacity. It was also used for rail grinding and had attachments for a snow plough. However, it was seldom seen on the streets, mostly working at night after ordinary services were finished.

The last tram ran on 31 December 1931 and within a few months of the tramways' closure all but two of the cars were scrapped, the exceptions being sold to South Shields where they continued in use for another decade or so. The sorry sight below left is at the Prestwick Road depot.

An usual fate befell car no. 23 – the last tram from Burns Monument on the last night. Its lower deck was purchased by the minister of St James's Church and was used as a garden shelter until after the Second World War. If not broken up, some cars, like the one pictured above right, ended up in other strange places such as in a field.

Newton Park School stood at the junction of MacCall's Avenue and West Sanquhar Road. On this card, sent in 1905, the recipient, Hugh, is told that 'this is the school your uncle was at. It is not a very good photo but [it is] a good school.' Over the years various additions were made, but the tower remained a prominent feature in the surrounding area. Initially it was a primary, but became a junior secondary before reverting back to its former purpose for a time before Newton Primary School opened in 1984. Thereafter it was used as a temporary home for pupils from the nearby Braehead Primary when urgent repairs were required in that school. During the First World War servicemen from Newfoundland were billeted there. Ultimately it became redundant and was demolished, the site being redeveloped for sheltered housing.

There can't be many football supporters of a certain age who haven't at some time collected cigarette or trade cards of players and teams. This selection shows some of the greats of Ayr United. Goalie Bob Hepburn signed for Ayr in 1926 and went on to represent his country against Northern Ireland, while fellow 'keeper Bob Smith played a big part in Ayr's Division Two championship win of 1936–37 and later played for Dundee United and Celtic. Half-back Andy McCall was a powerful player of the early 1930s. Inside-right Johnny Crosbie, a product of the legendary Glenbuck Cherrypickers, made his league debut in 1914, shortly before joining the forces. His talent was recognised and he later played a couple of internationals for Scotland and was transferred to Birmingham City. Hyam Dimmer, another inside-right, was a flamboyant and skilful entertainer of the late 1930s. Terrance McGibbon was a centre-forward who had the distinction of scoring six goals against Third Lanark. Another centre-forward, Peter Price, became legendary as a prolific goal-scorer in the late 1950s and early '60s, scoring 105 competitive goals in the two seasons between 1957 and '59 and averaging almost a goal a game in his Ayr United career of over 250 appearances.

Ayr United F.C. came about with the amalgamation in 1910 of Ayr F.C. and Ayr Parkhouse F.C. Somerset Park had been the home of the former, having opened in May 1888 with a 3–0 win for the home side against Aston Villa, while Ayr Parkhouse's ground was Beresford Park (off Beresford Terrace and where the ice rink was later sited). The new team's opening fixture was a 2–0 win against Port Glasgow. Over the century Ayr United's fortunes waxed and waned and at one time or other they played in all the Scottish major leagues (except the current Premier League). Major honours have eluded the 'Honest Men', although some would argue that the Ayrshire Cup victories over a certain other senior Ayrshire club come into that category! While the ground capacity of Somerset Park is now limited to just under 10,000, in 1969 at their match against Rangers 25,225 managed to cram in. There are currently plans afoot to move to a new purpose-built all-seated stadium. This would be changed times indeed for supporters who braved the elements standing in the open on the ash-strewn terracing and queuing up for Bovril at half time. Such were the conditions prevailing in the late 1950s and early 1960s when the following pictures were taken.

In this photograph, taken on 12 September 1959, the United team pose in a blue and white strip at the west end of their ground at Somerset Park. From left to right, the players are, *back row*: Ramsay Burn, John Paterson, Ian Hamilton, Jim ('Dandy') McLean, Willie McIntyre, and Billy Elliot; *front row*: Willie Fulton, Sam McMillan, Peter Price, Willie Paton and Jim ('Tottie') McGhee. The photograph was taken prior to a match in which the team beat Motherwell's 'Ancell's Babes' 5–2. Peter Price scored a hat trick and Sam McMillan and Jim McGhee one apiece. Jim McLean had an outstanding game, keeping Ian St John in check.

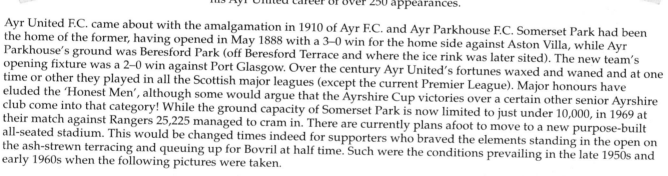

Right: Ayr celebrated their most famous giant-killing victory on 12 January 1957. Rangers were the visitors to Somerset Park in a First Division game and despite attacking for most of the game they failed to score. Late in the second half, Ayr broke out of defence for Willie Japp (on the right) to score the only goal of the game. Peter Price, beside him, shares his delight, while Rangers players Geordie Young and George Niven (on the ground) are left in despair. Ayr played with ten men for seventy-seven minutes of the game, Bobby Thomson having suffered a rib injury in a collision with Johnny Hubbard (who later went on to play for Ayr and did much for sport in the area). This was in the days before teams were allowed substitutes.

By 1960 Ayr United were still overcoming strong opposition in the First Division. In this picture Hearts, the reigning league champions at the time, have the ball in the net despite Willie McIntyre and Ian Hamilton's efforts, but the goal was disallowed for a foul on Hamilton by the Hearts player. Ayr eventually won 1–0 with a goal from Billy Fulton. The other players in the white shirts are Sam McMillan, John Paterson, and Alistair McIntyre – Willie's brother. Managers today must envy the crowds of 10 to 20,000 that turned out for these matches. The scoreboard gave half-time scores around the country after the interval, but you had to buy a programme to know which games were shown.

Ordered off! A black mongrel, having slipped past the turnstiles and upstaged the players for a while, gets its marching orders from the referee. Ayr were playing Third Lanark whose ground was at Cathkin Park on the south side of Glasgow. The club, which is still remembered fondly by its supporters, was wound up in 1967 due to financial difficulties. The covered enclosure at the Somerset Road end of the ground had not yet been built so local residents were able to view games free from their upstairs windows.

Ayr were less fortunate on 10 September 1960, going down 2–3 to Third Lanark in a First Division game at Somerset Park. Here Willie McIntyre is scoring from the penalty spot. The tiny dugouts in the white walls for the trainer and manager would not be able to cope with all the substitutes and extra staff required for today's games.

The Winning Post, Ayr Racecourse.

From time immemorial horse-racing has been associated with Ayr. At first racing took place on the sands, but in the eighteenth century a site was chosen for a course on the town's common, next to the road leading to the Doonfoot bridge and close to Belleisle Estate (the area now known as the 'Old Racecourse'). Throughout the nineteenth century the venue developed, particularly through the Western Meeting which was formed in 1824. However, by the early 1900s it was recognised that a move was necessary, the course being unsuitable for modern racing requirements (its tight corners were particularly dangerous). Land was acquired at the other side of town on the Blackhouse Estate and a new course laid out with stands and ancillary facilities. This opened in 1907. The picture, above, of the winning post dates from this time, while the one below (embossed with the town's arms) is from a postcard sent in September 1909. Some three and a half years later, in April 1913, the club stand was completely gutted by a fire started by suffragettes. Over the years additions and improvements have been made at the racecourse, making Ayr one of the most popular venues in the Scottish racing calendar.

The New Race course Ayr.